ANOTHER BATTLE TO WIN

ANOTHER BATTLE TO WIN

Making the Most of Life's Challenges

By Barry Kneisel

Copyright©2019 Barry Kneisel
All rights reserved.
ISBN-13:9781709727474

To my wife and best friend, Susie, your unwavering support allowed me to pursue my dreams. Your patience, kind soul, thoughtful guidance and selfless dedication to family have been a blessing for all.

And to Lauren, Drew and Alex who make life so meaningful, and whose character would make any parent proud.

Contents

ONE   Act on Your Dreams 1

   Breaking the Cycle 1

   Joining the Army 18

   Becoming an Officer 41

TWO   Believe in Yourself 59

   Getting a Job after the Military 59

   Surviving Cancer 71

THREE   Plan 91

   Preparing for the Military 91

FOUR   Live in the Now 106

   Army OCS 106

FIVE   Learn 120

   Lt. David 120

   Mitch 124

   Favorite Stock 127

SIX   Expect the Unexpected 133

   Mr. Bread 133

   Ranger School, The Desert 136

Ranger School, The Mountains 141

SEVEN **Be Positive** 147

Cancer Treatment 147

Military Chaplain 152

EIGHT **Learn to Sell** 157

Kai Blacktop Sealing 157

Kelly 163

NINE **Exercise** 173

TEN **Do the Right Thing** 177

Offerings in Equity Capital Markets 178

Fines in Equity Capital Markets 181

Army National Training Center 185

Conclusion 200

Recommended Reading 203

Acknowledgements 205

Preface

I sat in the hospital room getting ready to start day one of chemotherapy. There was a thirty-percent chance I wouldn't survive my battle with cancer. I worried about my children and how they would navigate life without the guidance of their father. I was most concerned about my youngest child, Alex, just 20. My two oldest children, Lauren and Drew, were out of college and had started their professional careers, but even they still had much to learn. Although I knew my children would probably roll their eyes at the prospect of hearing more "dad stories," I started writing down some of my experiences that might be of help to them as they moved along life's journey.

As I wrote, I realized that I'd conquered three significant challenges in my life. Each of them had helped prepare me for this battle I was about to enter. The challenges I'm referring to are not the ones you often hear about, those with straightforward parameters such as getting in shape to run a marathon or preparing to take a licensing exam, but challenges that took years to successfully overcome. Each involved personal sacrifice, physical or emotional pain, financial risk, and even risk of life. The challenge now before me was more daunting than all of the previous ones. The next year was going to be filled with uncertainty and the specter of death. Yet, I only envisioned success. My earlier challenges in business and especially the military had helped shape my positive attitude. Maybe others would benefit from knowing about them as well.

Snapshot

I grew up in a blue-collar town. Most of my family members had no formal education; they were manual laborers and they only made just enough to make ends meet. So my first major challenge in life was breaking out of my family and community cycle. When I was twelve years old I got my first job. It entailed waking up at 5:00 a.m. every day to deliver newspapers. From that point on in life, I would pay for almost everything I had or did.

Unlike my parents, I attended college, but I went close to home so that I could take classes while working full time. By the time I graduated (just barely, given my GPA), I had started six different businesses. Those businesses paid for my education, taught me the importance of a strong work ethic, and showed me how to take calculated risks. I also learned how to deal with failure. That alone provided me with some of my most profound insights.

A year after college, I moved to Chicago and began my first full-time job working for someone else – as a stock broker. Over the next seven years I worked twelve-hour days, including most weekends, in order to build a business. By my late twenties, I was earning an income the majority of Americans would never achieve. As young as I was, I had succeeded in breaking the cycle into which I had been born.

Then in 1991, following Saddam Hussein's invasion of Kuwait, President Bush deployed over 100,000 U.S. troops for Operation Desert Storm. I had a great friend in the Marine Corps Reserves who was one of those troops. He and I both wondered if he would be making it back home. His deployment was the spark that set into motion a dramatic change to my life plan.

After a decade of resolute actions to build a career and financial security, I abandoned all I had achieved for a new journey. Growing up during the Carter and Reagan years, I had developed a strong sense of respect and appreciation for the United States of America. Though my life's quest was one of financial success, I believed that everyone should give something back to their country. For me, that meant joining the military. Given that my age prohibited me from joining the Marines, my eyesight prevented me from being a pilot in the Air Force, and I lacked interest in the Navy, the Army became my top choice. The most challenging program the Army offered at the time was the Rangers, so I enlisted in the Army with the goal of becoming an Army Ranger.

I was 31 years old and almost everyone thought I was nuts. My wife of five years had had no indication this would be her destiny. We went ahead, though, and I spent the next two years at Ft. Benning, GA while my wife and first child lived in Atlanta. As you can imagine, Susie was less than thrilled about being alone as a first-time mom, but she stuck with me and I went on to train virtually non-stop at one infantry-oriented school after another. During this period of intense training, I rarely saw my wife, family, or civilian friends.

Being a decade-plus older than my military peers, I was often referred to as "grandpa" or "pop," but my age did not set me apart as far as training was concerned. At Ft. Benning, I jumped out of airplanes at Airborne School, set up landing zones at Pathfinder School, and learned to be an infantry officer at OCS (Officer Candidate School) and Infantry Officers Basic Course. I became conversant with mortars and Bradley Fighting Vehicles. The infantry training culminated with graduation from Ranger School, and afterwards I went to work at the 75th Ranger Regimental Head Quarters for a brief period before joining my assigned infantry unit.

I then spent the next two years with the 24th Infantry Division at Ft. Stewart, located south of Savannah, GA. There we trained daily in the stifling, humid heat of the deep South. Sometimes we prepared for desert warfare by training in the deserts of Southern California, or overseas in the Middle East. By the time my active duty military career ended, I was a battalion scout platoon leader. As scouts, we were the tip of the spear, the eyes and ears of a 600-man infantry battalion.

The day I signed my military enlistment contract four years prior, my dream had been to serve my country and become an Army Ranger. I had pursued and accomplished my dream. I'd spent four good years as a Ranger-qualified infantryman, serving both as an enlisted soldier and as an officer.

In January of 1996, I thought I would be transferring to the 1st Ranger Battalion, located at Hunter Army Airfield in Savannah. But now having two very young children and having been home only one third of the time, my wife and I made the bittersweet decision that my four years of active duty had been enough. In terms both of my career and financial well-being, I was about to confront the next major obstacle of starting over from ground zero at the age of 36.

Foresight might have suggested that getting a great job given all my years of diverse experience would be easy, but that was not the reality. I was consistently told that I did not have the current financial skill set or relationships needed for the specific job I wanted – work in the financial industry. Finally, through persistence, I got a job with a small firm in Atlanta. The pay wasn't great for the industry, but it was better than the military and substantially more than my offer to work for free.

Finding the optimal situation took two years and close to 1000 rejections before I finally secured a job offer doing the same role but at a much larger and better firm. My age, not having an MBA, and not having graduated from a "great college" were some of the many hurdles that I had to overcome.

I spent the next 18 years working in the larger firm's Equity Capital Markets division and ultimately managing their Midwest Institutional Equity Sales team. I was fortunate to be working with great peers and interacting with some of the smartest and nicest people on Wall Street. Furthermore, I was financially much more successful than my best pre-Army years as a stockbroker. I'd overcome another major life challenge. But the fourth was just about to begin. It would be my most significant hurdle to overcome.

For me, mission accomplished would be if our kids learned enough from my battles to help them achieve their dreams or overcome their own life challenges

ONE

Act on Your Dreams

Breaking the Cycle

Picture yourself being raised in a family and community where formal higher education was uncommon and manual labor was expected. To break out of that cycle required a strong belief that I would be successful, and the commitment to take action even when the risk of failure was high.

In Middletown, Ohio, a blue-collar, steel-dominated town, an 18-year old could make more money working at the local mill than what their high school teachers were being paid. It would take years for most college graduates to earn what the average steel worker could make right out of high school. Many would forgo acting on their dreams given the allure of high paying jobs as welders, pipe fitters, and boiler makers. In 1982, Armco Steel was the 4th largest steel company in the world. Their Middletown plant employed over 5000 workers, about one-third of the town's adult population. The sprawling facility stretched for miles, billowing smoke and steam 24-hours a day from its red-hot blast furnaces. There they manufactured the flat rolled steel that was used to make cars, trucks, or the guardrails that lined our nation's highways.

Work at the steel plant was hard, dirty, physical labor and at times dangerous. My Uncle Kenny was one of several relatives who was employed at Armco. One day he was standing near a flatbed truck that had rolls of steel chained to its bed. No one knows how it happened, but one of the chains broke and a heavy roll of steel fell off the truck and ran over

ACT ON YOUR DREAMS

his foot. His steel toed work boot failed to protect him and he lost all his toes. Painful and sad, but he knew it could have been worse because worse accidents had happened to others.

As a blue-collar industrial town, almost everyone was middle class at best or even dirt poor. There were a few upper-middle class professionals who supported or managed the working man, and a mere handful of the 50,000 residents would be considered wealthy. A few years ago, I drove my daughter, Lauren, around town and after fifteen minutes of silence, her only response was "OMG dad, I had no idea this is what Middletown would be like." What she saw was dreary and depressed.

Similar to the vast majority of the town's residents, neither of my parents or grandparents and few if any of my relatives had ever been to college. My dad's grandfather came to the United States in the late 1800s and was a grave digger. My mom's parents were born in the hills of Kentucky, my grandmother being one of 13 kids raised in a dirt-floored farm house. Her first husband, my grandfather, was a gambler and moonshiner, and their marriage had been turbulent and brief. Meme, my grandmother, like so many others including most of her immediate family, moved north to find work. They all were pursuing a better way of life with employment in the factories of Ohio or Michigan.

They lived hard in other ways, too. When my dad was ten years old, his father caught him smoking and locked him in a closet which quickly became a hazy cloud of smoke that he couldn't leave until he finished his entire pack of cigarettes. Grandfather's discipline may have produced an effective lesson for some, but unfortunately not for Dad. He extinguished two packs of Marlboros every day of his life and passed away at the early age of 63 from lung cancer. Dad was obstinate and proud until the end, refusing to have chemotherapy which would have allowed him to live months longer than otherwise. Yet, his work ethic and humility were great characteristics to emulate and a common virtue among his peers in our town.

My dad followed in his father's footsteps and became an electrician. A couple of years out of high school, he got a job at the steel mill and also developed a second job working on his own sign business. He would put in an eight-hour shift at the plant, and then if he wasn't doing a double shift, would work another six hours on his sign business. Every Saturday he would get up early and work six to eight hours supporting his own enterprise. He would work 70 hours a week for most of his life. I don't remember ever seeing my dad read a book, but he was self-taught, and his experience enabled him to do any type of skilled labor. He had a strong work ethic that entailed physical labor and a high tolerance for pain. Countless times he would cut himself in the hand or smash a finger, but he never mentioned it or complained, and he certainly never went to see a doctor. He was quiet, proud, and stubborn, which probably came from his German heritage. We didn't see him that much given his dual employment, though he made it a priority to be home for our family dinner each night. Although our life's paths differed considerably, his hard work and dedication to family provided me with a model for adult success.

Given that my dad worked two jobs, we were fortunate to have more than many in town, but at best we were still a middle-class family. As a kid, and up until the age of twelve, I did not lack the basic needs, but I also never had more than necessary. I had a couple pair of pants, a few shirts, tennis shoes, a swimsuit and an outfit to wear to church. I was no different than almost every other kid in our neighborhood. Unlike today's culture, we only had four channels on the T.V.

and no internet. We did not know anything different. What we did have was corporal punishment starting in junior high school which included being paddled with a long and thick board. Even our basketball coach would paddle us if we missed more than one free throw during practice. I played sports, volunteered as a youth leader at the local YMCA, went to Grace Baptist church every Sunday and Bible School in the summer, and took a one-week camping trip to a different lake in Michigan each year.

At a very early age my mom, too, instilled the importance of work and had my brother, sister and me doing chores after school and every Saturday morning. For this we would get a three to five-dollar allowance each week. We could spend our money on candy or save it for birthday and Christmas gifts. By the time we were eight or nine years old, we had learned all aspects of home maintenance from scrubbing toilets, washing baseboards, and cleaning refrigerators to painting, bush trimming, and vacuuming. Basically, we were taught how to clean or maintain every surface inside or outside the house. It was a lot of work, but a great early lesson in life regarding manual labor and taking care of yourself.

ACT ON YOUR DREAMS

When I was twelve, I wanted a new bike, so I got my first job as a paperboy. I would wake up around 5:00 to fold the papers that had been dropped off on our front doorstep. I would then ride my bike in the dark early morning hours, going door to door in our neighborhood to deliver the papers. Almost everyone in my neighborhood seemed to enjoy reading the Middletown Journal with their morning coffee. They were also generous with a Christmas tip to the young paperboy they never saw. Those were tips for which I was surprised and grateful.

Once I started the paper route, my dad must have decided that I was old enough to help him with his sign business as well. So, every Saturday when most of our town was still sleeping, we'd be on the road to one of his jobs. His business including fixing or replacing any broken lights that illuminated the billboards along the roads in the area, replacing burned-out lights in the local college parking lots, or hanging a neon sign in front of a business.

Dad's five-ton, 65' crane, or ladder truck, was usually our mode of transportation and the work platform we used each Saturday. I was his gofer, doing whatever he wanted at that moment. If I wasn't being the gofer, he would have me sit in a homemade swing that was attached to the end of the crane truck. There were no safety harnesses or straps to keep me secured in the seat. The swing was just an old piece of wood and two steel cables, and I held onto it for my life. Using the ladder truck, Dad would lift me 20-30 feet above the ground to replace a burned-out lightbulb in a parking lot or on a billboard. Yes, there were occasions when high winds would whip me around and I would crash into some metal structure high above the ground. But I never fell, with bruises and cuts being my only injuries. Accompanying my dad on these Saturdays, I learned how to wake myself up early, accept the realities of hard physical labor in inclement weather, and that pain would be a common occurrence.

Acting on my dream of achieving financial security began early in high school by adding cutting grass and shoveling snow to my list of jobs. My lawn maintenance and snow removal businesses started with work on one or two of my neighbor's properties every week when I was 13. A couple of yards expanded to dozens. I had my own truck by the time I was 17. During the winter, I used the truck to plow snow for the same clients whose lawns I tended in the summer. By high school graduation, I had enough residential and commercial jobs to warrant a couple trucks, a lot of equipment, and a crew of workers.

The lawn mowers we used were push mowers and only went as fast as we walked. We bagged the grass clippings and were continually dumping them into a truck bed when the bags became full. Cutting grass for eight hours every day in southern Ohio during the summer was grueling; temperatures reached 95 degrees in high humidity. I was always hot, sweaty, and covered with freshly cut grass. At the end of each long day, I would have to take all those grass clippings to the local dump or landfill, making the trip during peak heat and humidity when the stench of the city's trash heap was at its worst. When I got to the dump, I would jump onto the back of the truck and use a large pitchfork hoe to scrape the now steaming grass out of the truck and into the foul-smelling landfill mud. This revolting smell would remain seared into my brain until I was miles away from the city's dumping grounds

Back home, I would unload all the equipment and fix or rebuild whatever had been broken that day. Even in the evening there was no escape from the heat because few houses in those days had air conditioning. At night I would just lay on top of my bed with the windows open and sweat.

Hard physical labor in nasty conditions was just another day of work, and the lawn business provided a summer job for several friends. Besides earning money, I was learning that to pursue my dream of a better life required steady hard work, endurance, and perseverance.

During my high school years, aside from working to make money, I acted on another dream, regardless of the perceived obstacles and in the face of others' skepticism. I had played football for years as a kid but had stopped in junior high school to work. Our high school team was usually one of the higher-ranked football programs in Ohio. Most of the players worked hard for years to prepare, and many received college scholarships. Todd Bell ended up playing for the Chicago Bears, Butch Carter, who was an All-American in football, was known for his NBA tenure, and Chris Carter, Butch's younger brother, was an all-pro wide receiver for the Minnesota Vikings. These athletes were only a few of the many who obtained collegiate or professional success and came out of Middletown High School's football program.

ACT ON YOUR DREAMS

Despite the fact that I hadn't played the game for four years, during my Junior year, I decided I wanted to try out for the football team the following year. In pursuit of this unlikely dream I spent the entire year attempting to bulk up and build strength. There weren't any gyms located in my town, so I drove 20 minutes every day to the closest facility. I drank protein shakes, ate raw eggs, and consumed as much food as my body would allow, in a painful attempt to gain weight.

My Senior year, I showed up 25 pounds heavier and stronger than I had been the year before. I figured I was ready to participate in the twice-daily summer football practice. Both coaches and my peers thought my dream to play on the Varsity team was unattainable since I hadn't played in five years, but I didn't care. And in fact, I didn't play much that season besides on special teams; however, I did make the team, had a lot of fun, and started in one of the games - that is until the coaches realized that my skillset just wasn't there. The football experience taught me the significant lesson that it is never too late to pursue your dreams, but if you get off to a late start, you may not make it to the top.

Most of my peers had few if any real academic mentors, thus higher education was not a top priority. I don't know the percentages, but the majority of my high school class didn't graduate from college, though most of my friends did attend, many on athletic scholarships. Even without college, though, a high school graduate could make what was viewed as a small fortune at the time working at the steel plant. Not having much, just getting by, lacking mentors, and being able to earn a great income working at the plant, made breaking out of the Middletown cycle a challenge for all. But I kept my head down and plodded forward. If nothing else, I had ambition and the willingness to try.

I went to a nearby college, Miami University, a thirty-minute drive from my house. I would attend class, then drive to work on the lawn business each afternoon in the spring and fall. My college experience was very different from the one my own children had. I had a full-time job twenty miles away from the campus and dorms, and that job sometimes conflicted with the occasional class and cramming before each test. During the winter, if we had more than two inches of snow, I would drop all thoughts of class and studying, go home, and plow snow for the entire day or night. Spending more time working than attending class and studying had an impact not only on my social life but also on my GPA. I got through college, but I'm not sure I had the optimal experience.

Dad had a keen understanding of business and great intuition regarding new innovative ideas. Unfortunately for him, most of these ideas were years ahead of their acceptance. He was also willing to act on his ideas and accept the associated risk. When I was in college, Dad came up with the idea of using ultraviolet lightbulbs to allow people to tan themselves in a customized bed. We opened a business at Miami University called the "Tanning Salon," a concept which was ten years ahead of its eventual acceptance. That experience resulted in my losing over a year of income from my lawn service, but it provided me a painful taste of failure that motivated me to bypass future disasters.

I met Susie Elkins, my wife to be, during my senior year, and her first of many positive influences would quickly make an impact on my life. At the time, I didn't think I needed to finish school or that a college degree was necessary to be successful. After all, I'd started several businesses by then and saw that I could, indeed, make money. But she walked me through the pros and cons of thinking big and convinced me on the importance of finishing school and getting my degree, even if it meant taking summer classes. Her parents both had graduate degrees, one with a PHD in chemistry and the other a law degree. To them education and a degree were priorities, and Susie understood better than I what was at stake. We probably would never have married had I not obtained my degree, and my life would surely have headed in a different direction if I hadn't listened to her and acted on her advice.

Unbeknownst to me at the time was that Susie would become my biggest supporter and the critical component of all the future battles that I would face in life. So, in both of my senior year semesters, I carried full loads with twenty credit hours of core curriculum in each. After my peers graduated and left Miami, I attended summer school in order to finally graduate. But I did it. I became the second person in my entire family tree, after my sister, to earn a degree. My triumph was not exactly straightforward, but with perseverance and some good advice from Susie, I broke out of the indifference to formal education that was part of the cycle of my Middletown family.

Around this time, I met my first real mentor, Al Mistler who was then retired. I had been cutting his yard for years. I knew he was one of Armco's top executives, but I'd never spoken with him. One day he came outside his house, struck up a conversation, and invited me for lunch at a later date. Al had started in sales, but shortly after the start of his career, he took a four-year leave of absence to serve in WWII. He ended his career reporting directly to the Armco CEO. In some ways he had made it to the top, but he once said if it weren't for World War II, he might have been the CEO, himself. Like so many other patriots of the 1940s, Al spent a few years risking his life in the military to do his part for the country versus pursuing his own dreams.

Al was a wealth of knowledge, and his keen insight would provide an outstanding sounding board for years. We spent hours over lunch or dinner, talking about business, the stock market which he loved, and life in general. He was instrumental in steering my life in a different direction, much faster than it would have been otherwise. He guided me to pursue a career in finance as a stock broker. I was twenty-three years old at the time. His wisdom and breadth of knowledge prepared me for my future interviews and career. He taught me how to sell myself to the finance industry, which enabled me to get a job in an industry where the average age was twice mine. Acting on Al's suggestion would take me a step closer to fulfilling my dream of financial independence and security. His guidance would influence several decisions in my life, including the importance of having a good character and giving something back to society or others in need.

Becoming a stockbroker with a reputable firm at 23 was not the typical career path. The average age for brokers was 40 and most had several years of financial or sales experience before becoming licensed. I moved to Chicago where Susie lived, searching for employment: I spent several months trying to convince each firm that passion and work ethic superseded age and lack of experience. Finally, after being rejected at every firm I had approached, one gave me a conditional offer. Rich at a large national firm said he would hire and license me, but only if I successfully passed a two-week trial period. I would have to cold call hundreds of people each day for his top broker. I passed their test and became a licensed broker six months later.

As a stockbroker at two large national firms in Chicago, my typical work week was 60-70 long hours, cold calling hundreds of people on the phone every day, every night, and on Saturdays. My ambition was to build a business, and my goal each day was to talk to 100 people. I knew that 99 of them would say "No interest" or hang up. All these years later, I still remember one gentleman's comments to me as soon as he heard I was a broker: "Why don't you take a flying (expletive) leap through a flaming (expletive) donut," and then he hung up. Regardless of the verbal abuse I constantly received for invading their privacy, I usually got one person each day to invest in a safe municipal or corporate bond that gave them a better yield than their other choices. That one new and potentially long-term client that I obtained each day made the daily grind and pain of rejection an overall positive experience. For years, my life consisted of work and sleep, with little to no exercise or social life. I was conscious at an early age that sacrificing some of the joys of life due to work, constant rejection, and repeated failures were required if I wanted to be successful.

During this period, I'd married Susie, my college girlfriend, who already had and would continue to have, a significant impact on my life. Fairly quickly, we had a nice house and cars that we paid for in cash. We took great vacations, amassed savings, and had no debt other than our mortgage. We lived a comfortable life, with few worries. Our future was set, as my income and our savings/investments continued to grow every year. By the time I turned thirty-years-old, most would say I had succeeded. I had done what the majority of people, including my parents and relatives, would never financially accomplish in a life time. I was working at my second large national firm and had put in seven years of working 60+ hours a week. I'd been in the top one-percent of Americans in regard to annual income for years.

Starting very early in my life, I understood that it's not enough to wish for something. It's important to have a dream, but that's not enough. Taking action, working hard, and persevering to pursue that dream allowed me to break the cycle of modest expectations into which I had been born.

Joining the Army

What would most people think if a successful, prematurely gray-haired thirty-two-year-old, established in his career after years of hard work and on the cusp of starting a family, decided to give up his career and enlist in the Army? Crazy? A total head scratcher? As an enlisted infantry grunt, his peer group would be baby-faced 18-20-year old boys who only talk about girls, cars, music, and getting drunk. Thinking of this 32-year old who wants to abandon the secure and the known for the literal dangers of the military as well as the more theoretical dangers of the unknown, many observers would conclude there had to be more to his story. But in my case, there wasn't. I was simply another person taking action to fulfill a dream.

As we are growing up, almost every one of us has been told by a teacher, coach, or parents to follow our dreams. If we are lucky, they've said, we might have a career doing something we truly enjoy or believe in passionately. But by the time we reach adulthood, many of us come to think that we have missed the window of opportunity to act upon these dreams of our youth. Some of us are held back because we have obligations such as a family to support, or we've become fearful of leaving a financially secure job to pursue an unknown. Yet the truth for many of us is that it is not too late and we are never too old to pursue at least some of our dreams. But to do that, just dreaming isn't enough. We must act.

My interest in the military started before I was even in elementary school. I spent quite a bit of my childhood playing games of Army. The neighborhood gang would split up into

ANOTHER BATTLE TO WIN

two teams and have apple or mudball battles behind garages or attacks from tree forts. Those games lasted until one of us got hit in the face or drew blood, which quickly ended the fun as the injured child went home while the rest of us fled and hoped that we wouldn't get blamed. Those games planted the seed of military conquest in me, and I dreamed about army life throughout most of my childhood.

Fantasizing about being in the military, I occasionally acted on impulse. One night when I was probably no older than seven, our neighbor Bob Bowman, who lived two doors up the street, was having an outdoor party. Bob owned the town's lawn and garden store and had an awesome backyard that could have appeared in a French version of Landscape Digest. Our parents went to the party along with dozens of other couples. My younger brother and I gathered all the apples we had left from that day's abruptly-ended neighborhood battle. Once the party was in full swing and all was dark, we used our driveway as a staging area for our attack. We thought we were lobbing a few apples high up into the air into the Bowman's party and all would wonder who was shelling their party with apple artillery fire. We threw a

ACT ON YOUR DREAMS

few, got bored, and ended up in bed asleep before our parents came home.

The next morning our parents woke us up and asked if we knew of anyone in the neighborhood who was throwing apples at the Bowman party the night prior. My younger brother was usually the first to cave or confess, and this morning proved no different. Within minutes we were told that the party ended early because Mr. Bowman had been struck in the groin with an apple and had to retire for the evening. Within minutes of our confession, we both were headed to the Bowman house to apologize, pulled by our mom the entire way. Mrs. Bowman, who was one of the nicest people in the neighborhood, answered the door. Before the door was all the way open, we confessed and asked if we could also apologize to Mr. Bowman. She accepted our apology but said Mr. Bowman had been upstairs in bed since the previous night's attack, with an ice pack on his private parts to reduce the swelling. He would not be able to see us. We weren't sure what all that meant but knew it didn't sound good and that we were going to be in even more trouble than we'd originally thought. Yes, we were both punished with some form of spanking and given a multiday time out. This escapade was driven by my Army-fantasy and only one of many poor decisions I made as a youth.

One Saturday in high school, a group of us watched the movie *Patton*. We then drove a jeep through the mud, reenacting the scenes and spouting out the great one-liners of the movie. That day ended with the jeep firmly buried above the axels in a thick, black, mucky pit. Unlike in the movie, we didn't have enough people to push it free, and I had to pay for a tow truck to pull the jeep free of the muck. Later in college, a group of us would go to a nearby forest, split up into teams, and have bottle rocket or flying firecracker battles. The bug for the military was always present in me, but since no one in my family had ever served and I didn't know anyone who had served, I never gave joining the military a thought.

Sometimes people remember the catalyst that made them act on a dream. For me there were two distinct events that occurred within a couple of months of each other. In the summer of 1983, I drove to downtown Chicago with Susie to watch what were either the Thunderbirds or Blue Angels buzz up and down Lake Michigan with their amazing aerial acrobatics. The goosebumps were tingling up the back of my neck, and at that moment, I wanted to be a pilot in a fast-moving attack aircraft. A couple of months later in October, a group of us were having lunch in our brokerage firm's break room and watching the United States invasion of Grenada unfold. The Marines and Army Rangers were rescuing the American medical students who were in harm's way on the island nation. For days the media showed footage of thankful medical students exiting military aircraft, dropping to their knees, and kissing the American soil beneath them. At that moment, I knew there was more to life than making money. I believed then and continue to believe that everyone should serve their country in some capacity. Going into the military became a real goal for me, not just a youthful fantasy.

I spent the next several weeks researching how I could become a military pilot. The Navy and Marine Corps both had aviation branches with attack aircraft. They were also the only branches of the military at the time that offered a ten-week Officer Candidate or OCS program. Here civilians could enter military service, and upon completion of OCS, commit to four years of service, or decline the commission to become an officer and just go home. But the Marines were in a league of their own when it came to training their officers and enlisted soldiers. All Marines, once they were finished with Boot

Camp, become part of a cohesive team of intense warriors, focused only on accomplishing their mission. At the age of 25, I had applied for the Marines OCS program to become a pilot and fly those awesome jets. Unfortunately, I was rejected due to my eyes being a quarter of a quadrant away from perfect 20/20 eyesight. Initially I was bummed, but that feeling eventually faded as I realized being an infantry officer in the Marines would be a unique challenge. I reapplied to the Marine OCS program a second time and was accepted to be an infantry officer candidate.

My boss at the brokerage firm was more than understanding, relaying that he had always wanted to serve but had never acted on his interest. He gave me a leave of absence in case I was injured or decided not to take the Marine commission. I stored my personal items, had a farewell party, and drove to Quantico, VA for Marine Corps OCS. At this point in my life, I didn't know enough to believe this was my passion or dream, but similar to joining the high school football team late in life, I acted and pursued an interest with no reservations or concerns.

Quantico, VA is a massive Marine base located in wooded, hilly terrain about 60 miles south of Washington, D.C. Nestled in a remote corner of the base and adjacent to the Chesapeake River, was where the Marine Corps conducted OCS. Before I arrived, I had spent a couple of months preparing physically with three-mile runs and thousands of pushups, pullups, and sit ups. As much as I had prepared, after 48-hours in the program, I knew it hadn't been enough. The movie *Full Metal Jacket* wouldn't be released until two years later, but the first half of that movie is a great depiction of Marine training. The movie is very similar to the experiences I witnessed at OCS. Over half of our class were enlisted Marines who all knew what to expect, yet they struggled each day of the course, just like the rest of us civilian Marine candidates.

Every day was the same intense daily grind. We woke up early after a night of little sleep and had 10 minutes to use the head, or toilet, shower, and shave. Then we ate breakfast at nearby Bobo Hall, which was named after a Vietnam Medal of Honor awardee. After chow, we marched to a Quonset hut building for a couple hours of classroom instruction. The classes were fascinating, but it was a major challenge for me and others to stay awake after no sleep and our recent breakfast. We drank canteens of water until our bodies were screaming to be relieved or we jammed pencils into our hands to keep from dozing off. After the early morning classes ended, we did intense physical training, followed by drill and ceremony or marching, with the day culminating in more classes. All the while, we were always given too much to do and not enough time to do it while enduring accusations of our repeated failures and the screaming anger of our Drill Instructors. Each night before lights-out included a barracks prayer to Chesty Puller, the Marine Corps legend of WWII and Korea.

The obstacle courses were a smoker on your cardio and designed for you to push your body through varying levels of pain. The most intense and unique course we ran several times was called the Quigley. This course was a combination of the obstacle course we ran every day coupled with a long run through the forest which included other obstacles to navigate. Upon completion of the obstacle course, we were exhausted with heart rates screaming close to 100%. Then we put on our web gear of canteens and ammunition pouches to start the second leg of this course. One of the obstacles on the course was a culvert pipe submerged in water. This pipe had a one-inch gap or opening to breath, but only if you scraped your nose along the top of the pipe. If you were claustrophobic, you had a problem as you were pulling yourself on your back through a narrow and dark pipe filled with water. It was fall, so the water we submerged our bodies into was very cold. We exited this obstacle with soaking wet BDUs and shivering, but quickly warmed up as we continued running the course. They told us in the winter they would have to break the ice. In the summer, they had to pull out any snakes in the water before candidates could enter the murky water-filled pipe.

The intensity of Marine OCS was unlike any experience I had ever endured in my life. Some civilian candidates, if injured, would go home, reapply, and try again at a later date. The enlisted Marines didn't have that option and if injured, they would return to their units where they might have to wait upwards of one year before trying again for OCS. For this reason, few would ever acknowledge when they were hurt. George Jorgenson broke one of his big toes, told no one, and sucked up the intense pain of each step until graduation.

About a week before graduation and commissioning, I realized that for weeks I hadn't written or called friends, family, or Susie my future wife. The Marine Corps indoctrination had been wildly successful. My only interest was in the Corps. This proved to be an issue as Susie questioned whether she knew me, and it scared her to think I was somewhat different from the man I had been. My training had changed me and maybe not in the best way. Not knowing that the intensity of my mindset at the time would subside, I turned down the opportunity to become an officer days before graduation. I left having only the greatest respect for those serving, and especially the Marine Corps. My Marine Corps experience had lasted sixty days. I had acted on my dream but did not have the perspective or wisdom to commit to four years of service.

I went back to my job as a stock broker, got married to Susie Elkins, moved to Atlanta, and bought a house. I continued dialing for dollars every day, 60+ hours a week for five years, to further build my business. During this time, I became great friends with another stock broker and his wife. He was a Marine reservist who flew Cobra attack helicopters, and his wife was a reservist in the Air Force. From listening to their experiences, I learned a great deal more about the military and the honor of serving. During this time, I had a recurring dream where I was in a camouflage uniform, deep in the woods and standing in the back of a military truck with a group of soldiers. Obviously, the dream of serving in the military was still in my system.

In 1991, I was five years removed from my Marine Corps experience, and my Marine buddy was being mobilized to go to the Persian Gulf for Desert Storm. His ultimate deployment to Kuwait and then the following action in Iraq was the spark that once again had me questioning my focus on making money. I still had the urge to pursue my military dreams.

I talked to recruiters and found out that I was too old for the Marines and that Army OCS was only for active duty soldiers. I didn't have an interest in the Navy or Air Force, since my borderline eyesight wouldn't allow me to be a pilot. My only option was to enlist in the Army. The Army recruiter said I was qualified for any job in the Army and I subsequently asked to see a video of the most challenging job they offered. He showed me a fifteen-minute clip of Army Rangers in training. I'm sure the Thunderbirds and Blue Angels are both outstanding recruiting tools for the Air Force and Navy, but for those considering airborne infantry, the Rangers in Action video was exceptional and would inspire many to commit to the Army.

ANOTHER BATTLE TO WIN

Military service, given the physical and emotional stress, is a young person's career, with two-thirds of those serving being under the age of thirty and the average age being twenty-five. The Infantry is an even younger person's arena, with an average age of twenty-one. Most people my age were long since done with their military commitment or getting close to completing their twenty years of service and about to collect a retirement check. Many would also be collecting a separate disability check due to the wear and tear on some part of their body. Almost anyone other than my recruiter who had a quota would have said that I was too old to pursue this dream.

I considered all the pros and cons. There were a few big negatives to my plan: I had little to no chance of becoming an officer; my peers would be 18-20 years old and I would have little in common with them; my pay would be less than one-tenth of what I was then earning, and Susie, my wife of five years wasn't prepared for being a military spouse. The positives were also clear to me and furthermore, I now knew more about the military and felt I was making an informed decision. I believed that I needed to give something back to society; the recurring dream was a sign and acting on it was the right thing to do. (Some people would also say that one positive was not having to take time each day deciding what suit or tie to wear to the office.) All considered, even though I had a dream and passion, almost everyone except Susie and one friend would say the odds weren't great that joining the military was the right decision. Disregarding the many skeptics, I decided to act. I enlisted in the Army with a four-year contract and the goal of becoming an Army Ranger. I would spend the next four years in the infantry sleeping in the mud and sand of some of the finest swamps, woods, and deserts in the U.S. and around the world.

Almost anyone in the Army, other than a recruiter, including mine, would tell you that the odds of becoming an Army Ranger are not high. Once I was in the military, I learned that as few as twenty percent of those who entered the service thinking they would complete Ranger School and serve their four years in a Ranger unit accomplished either, let alone both. Anyone assigned to an infantry battalion in one of the ten Army divisions could apply to attend Ranger School, which made getting one of the coveted slots to attend a challenge. Students also had to successfully pass their own unit's Pre-Ranger course just to be considered for attendance.

Then only about fifty percent of those soldiers who attended ever completed the course and earned their Ranger Tab. My Basic Infantry platoon had only two of the twenty with Ranger contracts, meaning they had either completed Ranger School or were serving in a Ranger Battalion eighteen months after graduating from Basic Infantry. The odds for me were not so good. But I never viewed it that way and only believed that I would succeed.

During the months prior to my military service starting date, I began preparing. I worked out twice a day to physically get in better shape. I talked to anyone I could on what to expect, and I studied the Basic Infantry training manuals. By the time I reported for duty to start this new career, I was confident in my physical conditioning but not totally sure of what to expect.

My new career in the Army probably started as it has for every soldier who ever served. I reported to the local MEPS, or Military Entrance Processing Station, along with the other new recruits from my geographic region. Those of us who were going infantry were then put on a bus and driven to Ft. Benning, GA. There we waited at the Reception Battalion for almost a week. This was a temporary holding site where we drew our military gear, had physicals, and waited for Basic Training to start. There was no screaming from the drill sergeants, and we weren't being thrashed with non-stop pushups; we were just waiting for our class to officially start. Those six days could have been completed in two, but it was our introduction to how the Army operated.

At the Reception Battalion, ninety-five percent of the men were 18-20-year-olds, but there were also a few men in their mid-to-late twenties who had prior service experience and were coming back into the Army with Special Forces contracts. These men were quiet, kept to themselves, and were mentally getting ready for their upcoming challenge. If they completed SFAS, or Special Forces Assessment and Selection, they would proceed to Special Forces six month "Q," or qualification course. Then if they were successful at the "Q" course, they would be assigned to a team, and if not, they would be assigned to a regular infantry unit. Only a couple of these men would ultimately join a Special Forces team, but all were acting on their own dreams.

Ft. Benning is the home of the Infantry and where the Army conducts the majority of its infantry-related training. It is a massive base, covered with a pine forest of rolling hills, red

ANOTHER BATTLE TO WIN

Georgia clay, and various types of weapon ranges and training areas. At night you could hear the AC130 gunships overhead and the buzzing grunt of their Gatlin guns firing onto some distant range.

Basic Army Infantry Training is conducted in one small section of this never-ending base, a place known as "Sand Hill." The area is one by two miles squared and holds five modern "starship quads" or barracks, each of which houses about 500 basic infantry trainees at any given time. For sixteen weeks this was our home, and almost all our training would be in the vicinity or a road march away.

Basic Training started with 150 of us loaded into cattle cars. These were long enclosed trailers used to shuttle soldiers around the base, and they packed us in like sardines in a can. They drove us less than a mile down the road to a large building which was our barracks for the next four months. There we were welcomed by a dozen drill sergeants in their Smokey the Bear hats, who yelled at us for hours: "You're too slow"; "No talking"; "Move faster"; "Don't look at me"; "Are you staring at me?"; "How old are you?"; "How stupid are you?"; "Do you miss your momma or girlfriend?". These were just some of the comments we all heard that day.

ACT ON YOUR DREAMS

The first couple of days we learned a lot about the military. One of the earliest lessons learned was to hurry up and wait for further instruction. Our further instruction almost always included doing a lot of pushups. We learned the importance of keeping our barracks clean, neat, and organized, with every item placed in a specific location. Wall lockers were never left unlocked, or we would suffer some consequence. We learned how to march, which the military calls "drill and ceremony," military courtesies and customs, and we started our military classes.

On the third day we took our first APFT, or Army Physical Fitness Test. The APFT incorporated a timed two-mile run and the number of pushups and sit ups performed in two-minute time frames. The night before the test, they concocted a lame reason to wake everyone up for a smoke session of pushups and sit ups. They probably wanted to ensure that collectively we didn't do well on our first test. Their plan worked, as only three passed our first APFT. A week later we took our second, with the majority passing.

After about three weeks of Basic Training, we were struggling as a platoon, which is probably right on course for the tear-them-down-and-build-them-up strategy of the military. Being as old as our drill sergeants, and having the highest APFT score in the company, Drill Sergeants Brice and Bendez fired our basic trainee platoon guide and put me in charge. I became responsible for the actions of the 40 soldiers in our barracks. We had been failing every inspection, leaving items unsecured, and generally screwing up everything we did. Our lack of discipline always resulted in more pushups and sit ups. I implemented some changes to minimize the suffering and focused the platoon on working smarter and as a team.

We had all quickly learned the NCO technique of acquiring or borrowing whatever you need; this technique included never getting caught, using the "borrowed items" only for an Army purpose, and then returning the items when done. We searched the building until we found more brooms, brushes, buffers, and wax, which we would use to aid our efforts in passing our inspections. We spent our own money to buy top of the line industrial floor wax, which would give the floors a higher gloss shine. We had soldiers act as roving guards to make sure our wall lockers were always locked and to provide us with an early warning when the staff was about to enter the barracks so we could all be standing at attention when they walked thru the door. All the while, during our barracks time, we were constantly cleaning or preparing our gear for the next day. We never failed another inspection or had any unsecured lockers or items.

After our graduation ceremony, since I was the basic trainee platoon guide, each of the forty soldiers in my platoon took a turn giving me pseudo "blood wings." In this case, that involved pounding my service ribbon with its 3/4" pins into my left breast. At some point near the end of this process my legs buckled and I was briefly on my knees. I was dazed but quickly back on my feet, my left breast bloody and numb. The time-honored ritual of giving blood wings is highly discouraged, though commonplace, and mine was soon complete. I now had a sore and bruised chest, but also bragging rights. This was the only time in the Army I was given the honor of receiving forty beatings in a row. My preparation for the Army had paid off, and I was named the company honor graduate while finishing second in the company on the APFT. I enjoyed the experience, even though the fun infantry training had not even begun.

Advanced Infantry Training immediately followed Basic Training and was a blast. We qualified with the M16 on stationary and moving target ranges, learned to throw hand grenades, acquired basic combat lifesaver skills, made lots of road marches with full gear, ran the obstacle course several times, completed the confidence course, solved numerous field problems where we spent days in the woods, slept under our ponchos, took rifle bayonet and hand-to-hand training. We had MOUT or urban combat training, practiced infantry battle drills, and moved at night with NVDs or night vision devices. In addition, our chemical warfare training included the use of CS gas to simulate a chemical attack. CS gas is a form of tear gas used for riot control. The gas causes your eyes to burn, constricts breathing and opens your sinuses to such an extreme that your mucus stretches to the ground. Upon hearing the words "Gas, gas, gas," we would don our protective masks which sheltered us from its painful side effects. We survived the gas house where they had us take off our masks and inhale the pungent aroma. There we remained until the coughing and mucus drip became too extreme for the majority of the soldiers, and they allowed us to exit the building. Hard as some of these challenges were, they left me exhilarated.

Basic Infantry Training sparked numerous funny situations, especially if you were a spectator and not a participant. The drill sergeants were all top-notch professionals, the top five percent of the NCO corps. They were well-versed in their duties, and most were quick-witted. They were masters of using humor, ensuring that none of us would ever forget a lesson learned. We did our best never to be on the receiving end of their unique mind games. Given our numbers and the situation at hand, it was easy for them to find multiple mistakes in our actions every day. At times, it was a challenge to keep a straight face during one of their unique teaching sessions.

One technique they used to reinforce a point they wanted to highlight was to assign pets for us to keep. Mr. Rock, for example, was given to a private who decided to pick up a rock on a tactical road march and without thought made a noise while tossing it into the nearby brush. He was given a large rock that weighed twenty pounds, which he was ordered to carry everywhere he went for days. Mr. Bread was assigned to a private who tried to sneak an extra piece of bread in the chow hall, and when caught had to carry the bread in his cargo pocket for days, where it got soggy and moldy. Mr. Pinecone was assigned to yet another private who for some reason had picked up a pinecone during a training exercise. He had to keep the pinecone in his pocket, and at the end of each day in front of 150 soldiers, he was ordered to pull out and salute the pine cone, simulating a change of guard.

Catching someone in the mess hall drinking his milk while walking resulted in: "Hey you! Don't drink and drive! What are you trying to do, kill yourself, you idiot?" Drill Sergeant Dills would reinforce the importance of light discipline and play the Smokey the Bear game. A flashlight or lighter can be seen for miles at night, which could compromise an infantry unit's location. He would take all of our lighters and then make us recite, "I will not play with fire, because I am not Smokey the Bear."

If Drill Sergeant Bendez caught soldiers talking while in formation, he would make them imitate race cars and shift gears with their voices. Drill Sergeant Brice caught a private doing something stupid and made him lay on his back in front of each platoon while shaking his arms and legs in the air yelling, "Raid kills bugs dead."

The funny comments were always quick and to the point: "Hey, Dumbo, are you as stupid as you want to be, or are you still trying?" or "Have you taken all your stupid pills for the day?" or "Are you an idiot or just stupid?" or "What are you

– a poster child for Jerry Lewis?" The comments could be cruel but at least they were memorable and reinforced a lesson to be remembered.

Near the end of training I was asked if I had any interest in OCS. I would be able to get an age waiver. I talked to my drill sergeants and wife and ultimately decided that becoming an officer, if I was successful, would be the best route to pursue. Prior to the course starting, I went to Airborne School and then worked at the battalion where I had just completed my training. At this point in time, I was pumped on my decision to act on my dreams and looked forward to the challenges of becoming an officer.

Becoming an Officer

Little did I know that OCS would be the most profound and painful few months of my life. There was no fun, ever, to be found at this course. The instructors did an outstanding job of weeding out those who weren't qualified and preparing the rest of us to become officers. OCS, at the time, was a four-month course. Other than one 36-hour pass during a holiday, we conducted the entire course confined to our training area.

We were not allowed to use the phones that were twenty yards from our barracks, and our only communication with the outside world was by mail. Only active duty soldiers could attend, so all were well-versed in the military; even so, only sixty-percent of our class graduated. As challenging as the Marine Corps OCS program had been, Army OCS was brutal, substantially more difficult. This course was a blur of daily sleep deprivation, harsh twice-daily physical training sessions, continuous physical thrashings, and non-stop emotional stress. The program had been brilliantly crafted and meticulously executed on a daily basis to ensure that only the worthy would be commissioned.

Upon completion of OCS, my swearing in as a second lieutenant was performed by my Marine reservist buddy who had deployed to Operation Desert Storm and started my "want to join the Army mission." I finally got to see my now eight-month pregnant wife, whom I had only seen for thirty-six hours the previous four months. Tough as OCS had been, I had now been in the Army for over a year and loved what I was doing.

After OCS all of us who were 11A, or infantry officers, would stay at Ft. Benning to attend IOBC, or the Infantry

ACT ON YOUR DREAMS

Officers Basic Course, a six-month program. I would be one of a handful of OCS lieutenants attending, with recent ROTC graduates comprising almost all of our company of 125 students. In addition, there were a few international students, with Egypt and Thailand being represented in our platoon.

IOBC was a gentlemen's course, calling for the exact opposite of the emotional and physical pain we endured at OCS. Our first official training day of the course was nicknamed the $1 million display. We went to a range and were allowed to fire any weapon system in the Army's arsenal. They had, to name a few, the M1 Abrams tank, Bradley Fighting Vehicle, Mark19 grenade launcher, and 50 caliber machine guns. They had piles of Class V, or ammunition stacked by each weapon, and NCOs standing by ready to assist. The only weapons system that we did not fire that day was the AT4, a shoulder-fired rocket.

At IOBC we had great physical training every morning. It was geared as a teaching tool for how to conduct different PT sessions when we arrived at our active duty units, but the training wasn't twice a day, and we weren't smoked with pushups, sit ups, or flutter kicks as we had been at OCS. We had endless hours of classroom instruction on infantry tactics and strategy. Given that sleep deprivation was not part of this course as it had been in OCS, we never had an issue staying awake. Our instructors were outstanding with a wealth of knowledge, and the learning curve for us ramped fast. Occasionally we would have guest speakers, and one that I remember was the executive officer of the 1st BN 7th CAV during the Vietnam War's battle of La Drang. Mel Gibson played the role of LTC Hal Moore in the movie *We Were Soldiers Once and Young.* The movie was extraordinary, although the executive officer's detailed description of the battle was substantially more graphic than we would see years later on TV.

We spent a substantial amount of our time in the field or woods training. We had long-range day-and-night land navigation, calling for artillery or mortar fire, weapons ranges, live-fire ranges, and a stream of missions and field problems where we would rotate leadership positions. In the field, our home was our poncho, and our bed was a second poncho tied to a poncho liner, which was similar to a thin blanket.

Like every military course or unit, there were instances of humor. Lt's Horton and Lifton were caught conducting a land navigation course while listening to music on their Walkmans.

ACT ON YOUR DREAMS

Their punishment was to hang upside down while hugging a tree, acting like Koala bears.

Lt. Booker wanted to watch the devasting effect of an exploding claymore mine spewing out its one-hundred BBs. One of those BBs from the back-blast effect shot into his face and lodged in his sinus. Early one morning weeks after the incident, he came running to formation with a baggy in his hand yelling, "Hey guys! It's no longer stuck in my face. I blew it out of my nose this morning. Take a look."

The lieutenants who grew up in the city were not used to walking in the woods at night and were petrified of the wild pigs or boars that roamed Ft. Benning's woods at will. They freaked out at the sound of every noise in the woods during night land navigation training. The boars could inflict serious injury to a person; however, they were also afraid of us and almost always ran the other way. Furthermore, we were more likely to step on a snake, get a poisonous brown recluse spider bite, or have a fire ant crawl in our ears while sleeping.

Over the course of this class, we saw and interacted with more than our share of snakes, fire ants, bees, and poison ivy. Imagine seeing a black water moccasin sitting on a rock in your back yard one day and then having to walk near that same rock, later at night. Lt. Kint and I were land navigation buddies, paired together to conduct a long-range, day-and-night course. We moved four hours through the woods in one direction during the day to find our designated points, and then came back through the same general area at night. During the day we crossed a small ravine with a creek running down the middle. Just before Lt. Kint stepped over the edge of the steep drop-off, I told him to wait, as there was a small water moccasin coiled up on a fallen tree right where he was about to step. We moved further down the ravine and crossed at a different point, but both of us were thinking about having to cross this general location hours later in the dark. On the route back, Kint mentioned the pros and cons of just using the off-limits bridge. The pros would be saving a ton of time and not having to potentially deal with snakes in the creek. There was a remote chance that anyone would see us crossing the bridge, and if so, they would never be able to identify us in the dark. But the overriding con was that going across that bridge was against the rules, an integrity violation. The discussion was over. I crossed the creek first, with no issues, but both of us were thinking about that snake the entire time.

ACT ON YOUR DREAMS

During one of our longer field problems, we spent days deep in the woods training. Murphy's Law was in play, and we had a trifecta of memorable incidents dealing with Mother Nature. During one of our day movements, we all walked through a swarm of bees, and several of us were stung multiple times. A couple of nights later we all woke to the sound of Lt. Rohtka running around our patrol base, screaming "Ow, ow, ooh, ow." Something had crawled into his ear and was biting him deep inside his head. He was sent to the hospital, and hours later they somehow removed a red fire ant from his ear canal. Earlier in the field problem, one of our ROTC lieutenants was in charge of our movement. He clearly did not know the distinguishing features of poison ivy, as he halted our movement and had us lay down for a security halt in a field covered with the pointy-leafed, red-veined plants. Most of us changed out of those uniforms that night and wiped down the best we could with diaper wipes. Days later, seven of us were so covered with the itchy poison ivy that we were taken to the hospital for shots. All minor events, but a field exercise to remember.

Live-fire exercises always produced a high level of anxiety, as we were all new lieutenants, and most were ROTC with limited experience in maneuvering with live rounds. On one of these exercises, Lt. Penny was positioned behind me, and his M16 rounds of 5.56 were impacting into the dirt about 4 inches from my head. This was one of the several times that I came close to serious injury. It was also a great reminder for me to be more aware of my surroundings and to always expect the unexpected.

Lt. David, Lt. Steven and I were the platoon honor grads, and just like OCS, Lt. David deservedly won the class honor graduate title.

After IOBC, I attended and graduated from Ranger School, Pathfinder School, IMLOC (which is mortars) and Bradley Commander's Course. It was May of 1994, and I was finally done training after completing one infantry-related course after another during the prior two years. Those twenty-four months had been a whirlwind of excitement, learning, continuous and diligent preparation, and numerous challenges to overcome. Taking a chance and acting on my dreams in the face of skepticism had been the right decision. The time spent researching, talking to the subject matter experts, and preparing physically had been well spent, allowing me to accomplish my goals. I experienced how the body and mind can endure substantially more pain than ever thought possible, especially if you view life just one day at a time.

My infantry and officer training complete, I reported to the 24th Infantry Division (reflagged and now known as the 3rd Infantry Division) in Hinesville, GA, 30 miles from Savannah. An infantry division was comprised of three infantry brigades, each with roughly 2000 soldiers. A brigade had three battalions of 600 soldiers who were commanded by a lt. colonel. These battalions were structured to include four infantry companies of 100 soldiers led by a captain and one headquarters company comprised of scouts, mortars, medics, communications, cooks and transportation. Each infantry company had three platoons of 30 men who were commanded by a lieutenant.

The 24th was a mechanized infantry division; thus, the infantry would have Bradley Fighting Vehicles or BFVs for protection and to ride into battle. Four BFVs were assigned to each platoon and each could transport six dismounted infantry soldiers in addition to the driver, gunner and commander. Their supporting firepower was welcomed by the infantry and included a 25mm canon which could destroy light armor upwards of one mile away, TOW missiles to destroy enemy tanks within two miles, and a machine gun with a half mile effective range.

At the 24th ID I was assigned to 1st Brigade, 3rd Battalion, 7th Infantry where I would serve as an infantry and scout platoon leader for two years. The unit's history went back to General George Armstrong Custer's unit after the Civil War and more recently was the hammer that destroyed Saddam Hussein's right flank during the first Persian Gulf War, ensuring a quick U.S. and allied victory. My next two years would be spent training and preparing for a conflict which never occurred as the war on terror was still seven years away.

Having just completed a year of leadership related training in numerous infantry schools, in addition to seven years working for different managers as a civilian, I had high expectations regarding the strength of the leadership at the 24th infantry division. I was surprised by what I experienced.

I was one of roughly 20 infantry lieutenants assigned to my battalion and responsible for the lives of 30 infantry soldiers. I knew that my battalion commander would be one of my primary mentors for the next two years and that I was expected to meet with him shortly after my arrival. In this meeting I would be counseled on his expectations of me and suggestions

ACT ON YOUR DREAMS

for success as a platoon leader. A month after my arrival at the unit, I was at the battalion's sole copy machine and a voice from behind asked who I was. I turned to see my battalion commander and relayed that I was his newest lieutenant. He grunted a simple "ok." That was our only interaction until another month passed. Needless to say, I was taken aback by his leadership style and unfortunately it didn't get any better.

The purpose of the infantry is to close with and destroy the enemy; thus, our primary task in peacetime was to train and be prepared. Therefore, when our battalion commander told a group of us that his S1 shop or the administrative paper pushers were the backbone of the battalion, we were shocked. Battles are not won with paper pushers, and those comments highlighted his priorities, which were not training. Accordingly, I was not surprised during our next holiday break when only 15% of the battalion was given a pass or allowed to leave the area. As officers we all remained on base and let the enlisted soldiers go home to see their families. Our battalion commander, the senior leader of the unit who should have been leading by example, used one of the passes and left the area.

Consequently, it came as no surprise how the battalion staff handled our bi-annual weapons qualification. These included live-fire exercises involving soldiers simulating an attack and moving very close to live rounds being fired by supporting infantry. The exercises were dangerous, and mishaps unfortunately occurred on a rare occasion. During my tenure, battalion leadership modified some of these exercises to eliminate any potential risk which diluted the effectiveness of the training. On paper we appeared to be trained, yet the soldiers had not experienced the intended training on how to function with live rounds being fired near them. Our battalion commander was shocked when a large number of soldiers in the battalion submitted 4187s, which were requests for transfer to another unit. Instead of having an AAR or After-Action Review to address the cause and develop solutions, he was upset and said his men were not being loyal to him. The pinnacle of this poor leadership was six months after I arrived when Saddam Hussein sent several of his armor divisions south toward Kuwait and it appeared as though there would be another conflict. Our battalion was the division's DRF1 or Division Ready Force and tip of the spear. Our brigade commander, knowing the strength of our battalion leadership was lacking, sent our sister battalion in our place. The lack of mentoring would be only one of many lessons learned on what not to do as a leader.

During my two years spent at the 24th, I was gone about one third of the time and spent little time with my family when I was home. Several times we spent a month in the nearby woods for a brigade FTX or field training exercise; on many occasions we would spend a week or two in the field conducting weapons qualification. We deployed to NTC or the National Training Center for a month of desert training and went to Egypt for three months of training. When we weren't on one of these training exercises or weapons qualifications, we trained on small unit tactics or in simulators depicting friend and foe.

A large percentage of the soldiers, myself included, lived off post and drove upwards of thirty to forty minutes each way. A typical day when not training in the field or deployed would be to wake up at 4:30 am, 6:00 am physical training or exercise, and then performing the events on our training schedule until 6:00 pm. In addition, most of the officer corps and senior NCOs would remain for another hour or two for meetings and administrative actions. Thus, we would be getting home around eight or nine pm, tired and grouchy. We had maybe one hour with family before it was time for bed and to start the process all over again the next day. This routine was a blessing, though, compared to that of the soldiers who served during the last decade and were deployed for a year in Iraq or Afghanistan. That said, our spouses would say our peacetime training was a challenge for them. In their minds they were single parents who were trying to raise a family on military pay.

The military magnified what I had recognized when I was a civilian in regards to one's contributions to society or the team. We all wore the exact same BDUs, including the same color of t-shirt and socks. The level of education, color of our skin, gender, eloquence of our speech, and even rank at times was irrelevant. What mattered was solely the character, actions, and contributions of each individual, and how they benefited the unit or team. You quickly learned who to trust and rely upon to accomplish the mission at hand. There were many times privates would be doing the job of sergeants and staff sergeants performing the duties of lieutenants.

The fragility of life itself is ever present when serving in the military, yet the soldier's immediate family is also constantly enduring their own challenges. The soldier must provide for their family on the military's pay which is a struggle for most junior officers who have kids and is very difficult for enlisted soldiers with families. Family support groups help immensely in the soldier's absence, yet only minimize the challenges of separation. The military spouse lives the life of a single parent who is constantly worrying if their partner will be injured or die. When the soldier returns home, everyone is happy and breathing a sigh of relief. Yet, they are also transitioning into an environment where the spouse has been in charge for months and not used to the soldier being home. Household duties redistributed, finances discussed, kid problems addressed, and reacclimating with each other can be hurdles. Given the intensity and duration of training, including the deployments, this cycle repeats itself over and over.

My four years on active duty would end on a high note with new battalion and company commanders who were both great leaders. I would also end my last nine months as the battalion scout platoon leader in charge of some of the battalion's best soldiers performing one of the most challenging missions, which was finding the enemy.

ANOTHER BATTLE TO WIN

Besides Susie, and a couple of friends, most people thought I was crazy to join the military at my age, and the odds of success hadn't been high. Furthermore, financially the decision cost us a small fortune in potential earnings, but acting on my dreams was one of the best decisions I ever made.

I came away from those four years with some clear principles for living:

Act on your dreams, even when you think the timing is wrong or the skeptics are plentiful and outweigh your supporters. Don't miss your calling or go through life with regrets. Life is full of risk, and to be successful, you have to take chances. It is never too late to pursue your dreams.

Research or analyze diligently the situation you are considering, which includes asking high achievers or subject matter experts for their thoughts. Then analyze the facts, prepare a plan, and mentally rehearse how it will play out to put the odds of success in your favor.

Your mind and body can endure more than you think. To be successful you will need to work hard and push yourself.

ACT ON YOUR DREAMS

When the challenges become exceptionally difficult, just take it one day at a time.

Evaluate each individual on their contributions to the team regardless of their gender, race, education or title. A staff sergeant who never finished high school could be contributing more to the success of your team than a commander who graduated from an ivy league school.

Appreciate a good boss or leader as they are not common, and strive to be one yourself. Your boss's actions determine not only the success of your team, but your daily attitude. A poor leader may be two or three layers above you, yet no one will challenge their decisions or are just focused on their own careers versus their team. In the military you suck it up knowing leadership will change every eighteen to twenty-four months. In the civilian world, poor leadership exists even at the companies perceived as being great. Don't settle for that. Think of your team first and do your best to mentor and protect them from poor leadership. If you find yourself in a bad work environment that tolerates such, make the effort to improve the situation, and if that doesn't work, look for a new job.

The life we live as civilians is blessed compared to the constant struggles of most military families. Embrace and appreciate the life you are living each day. Most of us take for granted the freedoms we experience, which are a result of the sacrifices of our military.

TWO

Believe in Yourself

Getting a Job after the Military

A great book to read is *Think and Grow Rich* by Napoleon Hill. Hill interviewed the world's most successful people of his era, including musicians as well as military and business legends. He found the one common trait they all shared was that every one of them passionately believed they would succeed. Most would visualize their success and the future rewards from their current efforts. Importantly, however, to a person they each experienced countless failures before they succeeded.

In January of 1996, I returned from two months of desert training in Egypt in the same area that German General Erwin Rommel had battled George Patton during WWII. Besides the great training, the highlight of our deployment was the one day we spent seeing the great pyramids. The pyramids were inspiring, for sure, but if you ever visit, don't let the local vendors talk you into a free camel ride. Once you were on the camel, they wouldn't let you off until you paid them a generous tip!

Over the prior two years I had successfully completed Ranger School; I had served as the leader of a thirty-man infantry platoon as well as a battalion scout platoon. A position opened at the 1st Ranger Battalion and I had the necessary skillset to be considered. For a time, this position seemed like my future opening up before me. Being a platoon leader at one of the three Ranger Battalions would be the pinnacle for any Ranger qualified lieutenant. As excited as I was about the opportunity, though, Susie was rightfully less than thrilled. She reminded me that my obligation to the military could be over in sixty days. We had been apart more than we had been together. She was pretty firm about it: I needed to redirect. I knew at some level that she was right.

Military service is not compatible with spending time with family or earning a good income. Always being away from home puts stress on the family, and no one joins the military for the money. Visualize yourself raising a family and your job only allowed you to be home on the weekends. During my four years of active duty, I was with my family (which included two infants) only one-third of the time, and I was probably sleeping most of that. We had substantially less in savings than we might have had if I'd continued working in the finance industry: my pre-tax income from the four Army years totaled $80,000. I had no idea at the time, but I was about to face my third major life challenge and a string of failures.

Leaving the military at the age of 36, I would once again be starting over at ground zero. At the time, I believed my background as a stockbroker and my accomplishments in the military would quickly lead to a great job with a great firm. My assumptions turned out to be very different from the reality I experienced.

ANOTHER BATTLE TO WIN

After talking to several friends, I decided that I didn't want to start over as a financial advisor. The stock market had been strong for the previous three years, more people were investing, and many were watching the TV business channel each day for the hot stock. It seemed that the majority of investors were doing great on their own and believed they didn't need the advice of a broker. Engaging a broker had become passé.

I decided that the best course of action would be to pursue a career in Equity Capital Markets as an institutional equity salesperson. In this role, I would be involved daily with the stock market, with individual company or sector recommendations, and with professional money managers, not individual investors. At this time there were roughly 75 U.S. brokerage firms with equity research, sales, and trading departments. Depending on the size of the firm, they each employed between ten and one-hundred sales people. Almost everyone in this position had both an MBA and current relationships on Wall Street, neither of which I possessed.

I was consistently told that I didn't have the financial skill set or the current relationships required for a position in Equity Capital Markets. I made calls every day from a payphone on base to no avail. Finally, though, a month after leaving the military, through persistence, constantly selling myself, and finally "offering to work for free," I was offered a job in Atlanta with a very small brokerage firm.

The sales person is the liaison between firms, ideally developing a relationship of trust and expertise to leverage the client's time. These soon-to-be clients of mine were mutual fund companies, insurance companies, banks, corporate and municipal employee retirement plans, and investment advisors, to name a few.

I would be working in a specialized niche of the stock market. Picture a mutual fund you own or retirement account you put money in every month that invests in stocks. That equity mutual fund is actively managed by a team of analysts and portfolio managers or professional investors. They are buying or selling stocks in that portfolio every week and usually every day. These professional investors do extensive research on the companies they own and also rely on the seventy-five brokerage firms on Wall Street to aid them in their investment process. This segment of the industry is called the "Buy Side" and has hundreds of firms, each with their own research and investment department. They collectively manage trillions of dollars in equities or publicly traded stocks. When they buy or sell a stock, the transaction involves millions of shares which they execute with one of the many Wall Street brokerage firms, known as the "Sell Side." This transaction generates a commission paid to one of these brokerage firms for every share traded. Consequently, tens of billions of dollars in commissions are generated annually and the brokerage firm's mission is to capture as much of this business as possible.

The client's decision on which firms to use and how much to pay them can be difficult. There isn't enough time in the day for clients to deal with every firm. Thus, they only pay the firms they view as providing the most value to their investment methodology. Accordingly, some of the factors they consider to reach their conclusion begin with the quality and breadth of the brokerage firm's research: Are the brokerage firm's analysts right more than wrong and are they regarded as subject matter experts in the industry they cover? Does the firm have several good analysts covering many different industries? Furthermore, these professional investors want corporate access or the ability to meet with the CEO or CFO of companies where they have an interest. Hence, how

BELIEVE IN YOURSELF

often will the brokerage firm arrange these cherished meetings? Finally, the ability to execute trades involving large blocks of stock without impacting the stock price is critical to the client. The commission from these transactions is how the clients pay the brokerage firm for their efforts.

Imagine for a moment David versus Goliath or a division three sports team playing a division one team. These are comparisons of the disparity between the small and large brokerage firms on Wall Street. The small brokerage firm where I was now employed was at one end of the spectrum with 10 analysts who wrote research on one hundred companies in seven different industries. We had three strong analysts that our clients viewed as "value added." Our corporate access or the management meetings we arranged numbered less than one hundred nationwide each year. At the same time our trading desk was not efficient at executing trades at the best price. Consequently, my firm had little to offer clients so developing relationships while also adding value through unique stock calls would be the key driver to my business. In comparison, the large brokerage firm, where I worked before the Army was not one of the largest firms, but it had, in those days, over 100 analysts covering 1200 companies. This firm also arranged thousands of meetings annually for these same clients. Clients wanted coverage from this large firm's platform; the sales discussion was simply how much it cost to access it. The difference between small and large firms is significant, and therefore the challenges of working at a small firm were substantial for me.

At the small firm I focused on learning to be the best equity sales person I could be. I was assigned forty Midwest accounts to cover. Since I was the newest of the eight sales people at the firm, only two of those accounts had ever done business with our firm. I had a tough road ahead. I met with each of the prospective clients and consistently was told that since our coverage was limited, it was unlikely they would do business with us. Over the next two years I repeatedly met with these prospective clients; I convinced many of them to meet with our best analysts and called them weekly with information that would be viewed as value added. By the end of my second year the business I generated was 800% greater than my first year and over half of my proposed clients were now doing business with our firm. I had succeeded at the small firm and enjoyed what I was doing. However, I knew that if I was with one of the larger firms that had a broader base of analysts,

BELIEVE IN YOURSELF

more company management meetings, and a good trading desk, I would have the potential of adding substantially more value to my clients and making multiples of what I was getting paid, while working the same hours.

So, for two years I focused on getting a job with one of the larger firms which our clients would use daily. I called every competitor at least once and usually twice every month. My goal was to set up a meeting or at least speak with the head of the sales department. I was rejected over 1000 times during those two years. Failure was a daily occurrence. Management at these more prestigious firms thought I was too old. They observed (rightly) that I didn't have an MBA. Another failing was that I did not go to what they viewed as the right college. They couldn't grasp my leaving a great job at a large brokerage firm to join the military. They weren't comfortable with infantry soldiers at their desks. They just didn't believe my story and resume. They didn't even like my short Army Reserve haircut, (which Susie wasn't a fan of either). Frankly, it took a lot of grit not to quit in the face of all these rejections. But I didn't quit.

Having worked in the industry, I knew there was only a limited number of positions in equity sales in any given firm.

ANOTHER BATTLE TO WIN

I also knew that employee turnover at each firm was minimal. Both of these facts made getting a foot in the door hard. In addition, I had excluded New York City from the search, and New York was the home to the majority of those firms. The opportunities outside New York were few, and many of these positions were filled internally by someone from a different department within the firm.

There were a lot of obstacles to overcome; however, in the face of perpetual rejection, I never lost faith and was confident that I would succeed. Every day I pushed myself to improve my skillset and prepare myself for upcoming interviews.

My efforts to become a better sales person began on the first day and continued to my last day as I was continuously a sponge for knowledge. Specifically, I asked every sales person in the office, each client that I met, and even sales people at different firms what they viewed as the best attributes of successful sales people in our industry. I listened intently to what each person shared, even when it was obvious or repetitive. I emulated their suggestions to become better at my job.

In order to build relationships, I traveled extensively to meet clients and worked long hours to find value-added stock ideas for them. Consequently, I was rarely home with family, but I was able to develop the client relationships faster than expected.

Given the abundance of competitors all calling the same clients, it was a challenge for me to even get a response from many of the key decision makers at each firm. Hence, I was consistently having to think outside the box on how to make a connection and then develop a relationship. I'll share two of the many techniques I used. I would have personalized Ranger patrol caps made with the potential client's name embroidered on the back. I would include a handwritten note explaining the history and military use of this distinctive gift. Another approach was to send certain clients a great book that was related to a unique interest or hobby of theirs which I had learned about from one of their co-workers. Both of these approaches opened many doors and helped develop relationships with clients who had never previously acknowledged my existence.

To become more value-added to clients, I read extensively about the stock market, stock selection, and fundamental and technical analysis. I consistently asked clients about their approach to investing and the key factors they used in their decision-making process. I taught myself to think like a client so that I could add greater value to their process and not just regurgitate what our analysts were saying.

In order to find a new job with a larger firm, I skipped most lunches to make calls to our competitors, and I took vacation days to interview with them. Prior to every interview I did extensive research on the competitor's platform so that I knew their product as well as their most recent hire. Furthermore, I practiced answering every conceivable question I would be asked in an interview. Then, upon completion of each interview or phone call, I would do an After-Action Review and determine how I could do better the next time. These actions encompassed the majority of my free time, but as each week passed, I was one stop closer to finding a new job.

In May of '98 after visiting several times and interviewing with two dozen people, I was offered a job with a mid-sized firm in Milwaukee on their Midwest team. Over the next 18 years, the firm significantly grew their equity capital markets presence and became regarded as one of the best small and mid-cap research firm on Wall Street. Halfway into my tenure, I was co-heading their Midwest team and ultimately became the head. Every day I talked or met with the smartest people

BELIEVE IN YOURSELF

on Wall Street and interacted with outstanding peers. Weekly I traveled with the CEO or CFO of a Fortune 500 company. Financially, I did much better each year than my best year as a stockbroker before I left that business to join the Army.

Every day, you need to visualize yourself succeeding and think through what you have to do to realize your dream. But you also need to accept that you are going to fail and may even fail often. The trick is to learn from these failures, as the more you learn, the closer you can come to understanding what you need to do to achieve success. Don't fear failure. It's an important component in growth. Above all – never quit!

Surviving Cancer

Imagine going to your doctor believing you have a bad chest cold or the flu, only to be told that you probably have cancer and a few months to live. That was my introduction to cancer. During a ten-day stretch, my diagnosis and projected life expectancy changed multiple times. What never changed was that I had a cancer that you do not want and that I never wavered in my belief that I would survive.

ANOTHER BATTLE TO WIN

My ordeal started in September, 2018 when I visited my son Alex at college. I was doing pushups in the hotel room while he studied when I realized that I was getting winded, which was unusual. I blew it off as a chest cold until I got home, but the breathing issue continued. I went to see my doctor and she told me that I had liquid in my right lung, needed an X-ray, and should talk to a pulmonary specialist. Personally, I thought she was overreacting but agreed to the X-ray and skipped the specialist. After two days of phone tag, she finally left a voice mail and said, "Go to the hospital now. Your lung is half full of liquid. You need to have a CT scan. If you don't think you can make the drive, call an ambulance." She had a sense of urgency in her voice. Given that I felt fine, I disregarded her last words which revealed the gravity of my situation.

When I got to the nearest hospital's emergency room for a CT scan, Susie and I thought I had a touch of pneumonia. We were both laughing and joking, but our jokes quickly ended when the emergency room doctor entered our cubicle with a concerned face. Neither of us was expecting anything serious, so Susie jokingly asked, "So I assume that look on your face means bad news?" He slowly shook his head up and down.

Then there was silence, our hearts sank and our world was turned upside down. I would never forget that moment. He said I had several enlarged lymph nodes in my chest, and they were probably cancerous. He admitted me to the hospital for the night so that early the next morning they could run tests and make a diagnosis. Most importantly they would drain my lung. I never realized until then that your lungs extend to the top of your shoulder blades. My right lung at that moment was totally full of liquid.

That night I talked to doctor friends who tried to calm my fears by stating that there was a possibility that I had an infectious disease which was highly curable, or maybe even a lymphoma. I spent hours on the internet researching infectious diseases and varying lymphomas. The prognosis for lymphoma was all over the map, with some saying life expectancy was less than a year. I didn't find anything that was consistent or positive from what I was reading. My first night spent in a hospital included me on my knees praying that I had some form of infectious disease such at Tuberculosis. Susie, drove home alone in tears and in a state of shock.

An oncologist, came to my room early the next morning, and grilled me with questions for 30 minutes. He concluded that given my symptoms or the lack thereof, I did not have an infectious disease or some form of lymphoma. Both of these diagnoses were best case scenarios. His opinion was that I had a one in a million chance of this being an infectious disease. He thought it was more likely that I had a malignant tumor in my lung that was being hidden by the liquid. I asked what that meant, what would be the potential treatment, and what would be my life expectancy. He was detached and elusive but explained that they had several options if he was right. He acknowledged that I might have only a few months to live. This bleak prognosis possibly explained his aloof demeanor.

They drained my right lung with a procedure known as a thoracentesis, and my breathing returned to normal with no huffing and puffing from simply walking up a single flight of stairs. And they saw that I did not have a tumor as they had expected. I was sent home with an appointment for an operation to be performed a week later which would remove a tissue sample. Waiting to have that procedure was a bitch. All surgeries carry risk and I was informed that my lung issue coupled with the anesthesia would complicate this procedure. Thus, planning for the worst was the prudent strategy. I updated my will and power of attorney, but I passed on one

BELIEVE IN YOURSELF

person's suggestion that I write my obituary. During the surgery, they removed an inflamed quarter sized lymph node from my shoulder and performed a biopsy. Once again waiting for the results was brutal. We just wanted to know what I had, what that meant and how to attack the situation. Another week passed before Susie and I met with the oncologist to hear his diagnosis. He said he thought I had a very rare form of NHL or Non-Hodgkin's Lymphoma called Peripheral T-Cell Lymphoma. I would need chemotherapy, a bone marrow transplant, and, he said, their hospital system was not qualified to perform transplants. This procedure entailed not only finding a matching donor, but one who would endure the risk and pain associated with having bone marrow drilled from their hip. I would receive a high-octane dose of chemo to kill all my white blood cells which would reduce my immune system to zero. There would be risk of fatality for several days from just catching a common cold and until the new cells repopulated.

The oncologist's conclusion was that I had a fifty-percent chance of being alive in the next three to five years. So, after waiting a week for that great news, I was referred to another hospital, another doctor, and more waiting. At that point, all I had heard from our conversation was that I had a fifty-percent chance of surviving, which was dramatically better than what they'd thought a few days prior. However, unbeknownst to me, Susie asked her neighborhood doctor friend to look up Peripheral T-Cell Lymphoma and to give her an honest and professional opinion. Susie's friend made it clear that this wasn't her area of expertise and asked if Susie really wanted her opinion. The conversation ended with her walking home, choked up, tears pouring down her face, knowing that most likely I would not be alive in five years.

The following week I went to the new hospital, which was regarded as the best oncology center in Wisconsin. I met with my new oncologist who had spent time at Mayo, lectured at MD Anderson, and was known as the region's expert in Non-Hodgkin's Lymphoma and bone marrow transplants. Our meeting was not the typical doctor visit or what we had experienced with our first oncologist where emotions were avoided and time spent with me appeared to be rationed. The new oncologist was relaxed, patient, engaged, extremely positive, and optimistic that he could cure this disease. He said I had a seventy-percent chance of being cured, with treatment lasting upwards of one year, which included a bone marrow

BELIEVE IN YOURSELF

transplant. The biopsy was re-examined by the new hospital, and the new doctor concluded that the analysis of the original biopsy was wrong. They then performed a bone marrow draw, which confirmed that I, indeed, had a very rare cancer, though different form of NHL. I had T-Cell Lymphoblastic Lymphoma, which was similar to ALL or Acute Lymphoblastic Leukemia. This cancer had the same cure rate as the previous diagnosis, but if the chemotherapy was successful, I would not need the high-risk bone marrow transplant. I left the new oncologist's office not thinking about my upcoming journey and its potential perils, but only that I would be one of the seventy percent who survived and was cured. I also knew that I was fortunate to have found a great doctor who had an infectiously positive personality and great sense of humor. Over the following months I would witness firsthand the impact of a positive and optimistic attitude, yet also given the nature of cancer, the rarity of seeing these attributes in most of my caregivers.

Finally, after waiting for what seemed like an eternity, I now knew what type of cancer I had. I was one of roughly 800, mainly men age seventeen to thirty, who get this cancer each year in the United States. The doctors had no idea how I got this disease, but it was not genetic and simply a bad draw of the lottery. My body was filled with cancerous tumors the size of quarters, located near my major arteries and main organs. In my case, the largest cluster was in my mediastinum, which is the sack that surrounds your heart. Seeing an image of my heart surrounded by several large yellow cancerous tumors wasn't uplifting, but at least now I knew where I stood. My right lung continually filled with bile as a reaction to these tumors, and after ten days I had my lung drained three times. During this procedure the doctor would insert a catheter between my ribs into my lung, and then we would wait 20 minutes for a quart of orange colored bile to collect into a once clear jar. This would allow me to breath normal for a couple days until we had to do the procedure all over again.

Cancer and its treatment are profound, both physically and emotionally, with nasty side effects. I lived one day at a time, pushing myself daily just to eat a couple meals and perform some type of exercise. I only focused on what I needed to do to succeed, which included power walking the oncology center's hallways several times a day for 20-30 minutes. I would crank the volume on Spotify and drag my IV pole and its bags of chemo that were attached to the PIC line in my right

BELIEVE IN YOURSELF

bicep, weaving between the nurses and doctors who were conducting their daily rounds. Early in my treatment I would do pushups and sit ups in my room until the doctors relayed that hospital floors were a collection bed for the worst of germs - those that I needed to avoid at all cost. Before I started day one of treatment, and every day thereafter, I adamantly believed I would succeed. Each day, I would visualize my goal of remission and life without this deadly disease.

My treatment lasted one hundred and seventy days, with half of those spent at the hospital. Only once after my treatment did I briefly think about my 30 percent odds of death. A good friend used the analogy of my treatment having been a deadly game of Russian Roulette with two bullets always loaded into a six-shot revolver. Not having my aggressive chemo regimen would have simply loaded all the chambers. My process included one operation, a dozen transfusions, and twenty procedures involving long needles that were stuck into my spinal cord, lung, or hip. Though I did not have cancer in my spine, the spinal cord is a transit center from your brain sac to your scrotum, and a rapid carrier of cancer. My treatment included "Lumbar Pushes," or spinal taps where different chemo drugs were injected into my spinal cord as a preventative maintenance measure. Some of these procedures didn't go as planned and resulted in sharp zings, or bolts of pain, similar to hitting a nerve in your tooth with no Novocain. I received so many of these "Lumbar Pushes" that I developed scar tissue in two different locations on my spine, which a needle wouldn't penetrate. On those occasions the doctor would have to redo the entire painful procedure.

Bone marrow draws will make everyone's list of the "top ten things they never want to do again," and I was fortunately the recipient of only two of these procedures. The first confirmed the type of cancer I had and that I indeed had a small trace of cancer, or one tenth of one percent, in my bone marrow. The procedure to test bone marrow for cancer was similar to the "Lumbar Push" but involved using either a larger needle, or an actual drill and drill bit, to extract the bone marrow from my hip. Imagine seeing a small power drill with a large drill bit attached sitting on the table next to your bed, and then minutes later hearing the hum of the device as the drill is grinding into your hip bone. Unlike the other procedures, I gripped the table until my knuckles turned white and sweat soaked my forehead as I sucked up the pain.

BELIEVE IN YOURSELF

An interesting lesson learned from this procedure was that they were able to find the cancer in my bone marrow because of a new marker on an old diagnostic test. This marker was not available 18 months prior, and the doctors would not have been able to detect that I had cancer in my bone marrow at that time, underscoring the benefits of the continued advancements in today's medicine.

Chemotherapy regimens and drugs are different for each type of cancer. Some regimens are administered once or twice a week or month as outpatient procedures, and others like mine are inpatient.

The protocol for my cancer was eight separate cycles of inpatient stays at the hospital. I would stay there for four or five days each time, if all went well. During each of these sessions they would inject me with two of the half-dozen different drugs they used. The duration of each push into my body ranged from two to four hours twice a day, to a continuous 24-hour drip. Each of the main chemo drugs had a different impact on my body. The names of those used in my therapy were Methotrexate, Cytarabine, Cyclophosphamide, Doxorubicin and Vincristine, in addition to a steroid regimen given every other cycle. All the drugs were administered in conjunction with another dilutive liquid, such as sodium bicarbonate or Mesna, to minimize the impact on my organs. Methotrexate could have a damaging impact to the liver and kidneys resulting in death, while Vincristine caused ten percent of patients to have permanent tingling in their fingers or toes.

There was fatality risk during chemotherapy, especially in the early sessions from my body's organ reaction to the drugs and the effects of the cancerous tumors breaking down on my organs.

I had a general expectation of how my body would react to chemo, and I wasn't surprised, though I was not totally prepared. My first session in the hospital was supposed to be four days of treatment and one day of monitoring. But the hospital floor doctor ended her text book oncology in brief on what I could expect by relaying that they hoped to have me home within two weeks. They would monitor my reaction to the drugs and keep me on site, should complications arise. The doctor was surprised and appeared bewildered at the shock on Susie's face after hearing that I would spend two weeks at the hospital. This would be the first of several situations during my treatment to always expect the unexpected. The thirty-two days of chemo were accompanied or followed by another thirty-two to forty days of nausea and extreme fatigue. The nausea meant that I had no interest in food. That usually started on day three of treatment and lasted four to five days. I should have done more research on what not to eat, since the side effects from chemo therapy are mentally associated with whatever you just ate. I could not eat chili, or grilled cheese sandwiches, always two of my favorites, until six months after my treatment ended. In addition, the smell of the detergent used on the plastic lid covering my food was revolting. Eventually, I had to leave it outside my room, or I wouldn't be able to eat any portion of my meal. Everything I ate tasted as though I was chewing metal with my food. I tried plastic silverware, but that didn't help. The good news was the nausea drug, Zofran, minimized the side effects and allowed for some food intake. For a few days after each treatment cycle, the only food I could stomach was saltine crackers with peanut butter, or fruit popsicles.

Chemotherapy drains your body and has a cumulative effect, making each session successively more challenging. Think of having your worst flu where the symptoms remain for four to five days. My body was so drained, achy, and cold

ANOTHER BATTLE TO WIN

at the core, that all I wanted to do after each four-day session ended was get warm and sleep. I was always wearing multiple layers of clothes, including a knit cap which rarely left my head for over six months. Occasionally I would have to take a hot bath to get warm, though the cold feeling never entirely left.

My white blood cells would be taken to almost zero each session, which meant I had no immune system for several days. They called this being "neutropenic." If I'd caught a cold during this period, I could have ended up in the ICU and potentially died. Early in my treatment, I met a cancer patient who relayed how his friend, during a low white cell count, had gone to a restaurant, caught a cold which became pneumonia, and died. After hearing that story, vigilance and extreme hand washing would be a common daily occurrence for the duration of my treatment.

My red blood cells and platelets were under stress, and I needed multiple transfusions. When my platelets got too low, I would get bloody noses that wouldn't stop bleeding. I'd make a quick trip to the hospital, get a transfusion of platelets, which took about an hour, and then all was back to normal. The red blood cells being low provided less oxygen to my

BELIEVE IN YOURSELF

body, and after a few sessions were always slow to recover. When my red blood cell counts got really low, it felt like someone was always sitting on my chest. Then I would get a transfusion of blood, which took three hours. Power walking the hospital hallways and using the stationary bike or treadmill would elevate my heart rate to 90% of maximum within just a couple of minutes. The lower red blood cell counts would not fully recover for months and added to my overall fatigue.

The only time I wasn't tired during this process was when I was prescribed Prednisone steroids for a few days every other session. Regardless of how tired I was, the steroids gave me a burst of energy and made going to sleep a challenge. I quickly found out that I was not going to sleep much unless I took Melatonin. A couple of times when I was at home, I felt so great that I worked out twice during the day, forgot to take Melatonin, and then stayed awake the entire night.

Chemo brain was a constant issue, at its worst during the four-day chemo session but persisting throughout my treatment. The simplest act would take longer than normal to perform, as my cognitive functions were running two-thirds of what they had been pre-cancer. I continually lost my train of thought and had a difficult time focusing on any task. This made correspondence challenging as it always took an extremely long time to write replies to well-wishers. At times I would just skip sending email or text replies, due to the lack of focus or because I was too tired to think about a response.

When drugs are first introduced, the risk of allergic reactions is high and patients must be closely monitored. At the end of session two, I was prescribed Allopurinol. I took the pill the morning of my first day home from the hospital. By the afternoon, I noticed that I had dozens of red dots on my stomach. Later that evening, the dozens had become hundreds, and then thousands. Visualize your entire body covered with what looked like small mosquito bites. Around midnight on a Friday night, Susie and I drove to the emergency room, where we were greeted by an extremely large and diverse crowd of waiting patients. I sat away from the crowd with a mask on in hopes of not catching someone else's illness. It took an hour to have my name called, and then another hour to meet with the doctor. He concluded that I was allergic to the Allopurinol and gave me a steroid prescription, which eliminated the problem within a day.

Mouth sores from chemo are common and one of the most painful side effects of chemo. The doctors recommended brushing my teeth more than usual and also rinsing with warm saltwater. The pain from these sores was unbearable and I couldn't eat. Every swallow of food or liquid felt as if a knife was gouging the inside of my mouth or throat. I brushed and gargled warm saltwater at least a dozen times a day. In my seventh session, I got a sore in my throat which resulted in my choking myself awake with a throat full of mucus every few hours at night. Not the most pleasant experience, and a bit shocking when you woke up, but I knew it could have been so much worse. After the eighth session, just as I was thinking I was all clear, I bit my tongue and developed a sore. I couldn't eat a popsicle without excruciating pain. Magic Mouthwash, a mixture of Benadryl and Lidocaine, was prescribed and fixed the problem. The drug numbed my mouth and throat for one hour, which allowed me to eat and get some sleep. Once my white cell counts rose, the sore quickly healed.

During my treatment I kept negative emotions at bay and focused only on the positive. That said, near the end of my first week in the oncology center an event would trigger my only moment of negative emotion, one of sadness coupled with gratitude. I was cruising the hallways with my pole of drugs in tow when the doors before me suddenly opened and a team of caregivers pushed a wheelchair onto the floor. The occupant was a young man no older than 23 dressed in a sterile hospital suit with mask, goggles, gloves and hairnet. He was wheeled into the room next to mine which he never left during the rest of my stay. He had just received a bone marrow transplant. Prior to that moment the only time tears had ever swelled in my eyes was seconds after my father passed. Seeing this young man in his prime having to endure this battle for survival didn't seem fair; it hit too close to home and would generate my second set of watery eyes. I also knew I was blessed and thankful that it is was me and not one of my children or their friends who had been cursed with this disease.

What did I do besides spend half my time at the hospital? Be a hermit! I never forgot the story of the patient who died from catching a common cold when his cell counts were low. Over the course of six months, I rarely went outside unless I was going to the hospital. I only left the house or yard six times. Twice I went to see a morning movie with Susie and twice to the grocery after 10:00 pm when few shoppers were present. I shoveled snow a couple times and had coffee with a neighbor once. When my immune system was near zero, I was

BELIEVE IN YOURSELF

at high risk unless I was wearing glasses, a mask, and constantly washing my hands. Inside our house I was paranoid of someone leaving behind germs. I was constantly sanitizing the doorknobs, sink handles, TV remotes, refrigerator handles, and cabinet knobs. This extreme routine paid off as I never got sick and avoided visiting the intensive care unit. I was blessed!

Once I was done with my sixth session, I had a PETSCAN which displayed a 3D image of my internal organs. I also had a second bone marrow test to see if the cancer was in remission, which it was. I then completed two more five-day fun filled inpatient chemo sessions followed by maintenance therapy that would last two years. This included daily chemo pills, a monthly chemo injection, and a quarterly "Lumbar Push" to ensure that the cancer does not recur.

Six months after my eighth and final session I was still cancer free and had passed the highest risk period of recurrence. Best of all, my hair had grown back and my appetite for all types of food had returned. In hindsight, this ordeal was a greater battle than I expected, yet nothing compared to what others have endured, especially so many of our veterans.

ANOTHER BATTLE TO WIN

I attacked cancer the same way I approached other life challenges. I believed I would succeed and every day would visualize being cancer free. I would picture myself being healthy, having hair once again, eating normal meals, and having a beer.

A support system is critical to success in any long battle or life challenge. Trying to go it alone is fraught with risk and low odds of success. At a minimum you need one strong, vocal and inspirational supporter for that string of days when nothing goes right. I had Susie who was my biggest supporter in this fight and every battle prior.

There were several occasions I briefly questioned my survival but quickly pushed aside any negative thoughts. During these periods, I immediately refocused on the passionate belief in my ultimate success. This in turn reinforced only positive thoughts and actions which allowed me to continue pushing myself every day. I view my die-hard belief in being able to beat this disease as the cornerstone that enabled me to become cancer free.

Never quit!

Never stop believing in yourself and every day visualize your ultimate success.

THREE

Plan

Preparing for the Military

The day I decided to exchange a suit and tie for the military battle dress uniform, I was told that my only option was as an enlisted soldier. The Army's OCS program was only for active duty soldiers, which I clearly wasn't. In addition, given my advanced age of thirty-one years, I was also too old for OCS. My recruiter informed me that considering my Army entrance exam scores, I could do anything I wanted excluding Special Forces, which was only for active duty or enlistees who had prior military service. I asked to see the most challenging program they offered and was shown a video of Army Ranger Training. Jumping out of airplanes and helicopters, rappelling face forward down a 100-foot mountain cliff, moving with night vision devices through a thick forest or swamp in the dark of night were some of the inspirational highlights. They sealed my fate.

To accomplish my goal of becoming an Army Ranger, I needed a detailed plan that physically and mentally prepared me for the unknown, unexpected, and extreme situations that I would face. My plan would be repeatedly challenged over the next eighteen months. The ultimate test of the plan would be when I successfully completed one of the Army's most difficult courses – Ranger School.

Ranger training does not compare in intensity to the Navy Seals BUDS course, from what I've learned. That said, Ranger School is one of the best leadership schools in the world, grueling, with a high failure rate and risk of serious injury or death. The course also requires the ability to function at a high level with little to no sleep or food for days. At the time,

PLAN

Ranger School was seventy-three days long, broken down into four very challenging and unique phases. The first phase was administered at Ft. Benning, GA. This phase was the indoctrination, or weed out, phase that tested our physical endurance and mental drive while under stress.

First, to evaluate our physical fitness we performed the standard Army Physical Fitness Test, which was evaluated at a higher standard than normal and included having to do dead hang pull ups. Next was a five-mile, forty-minute formation run while dressed in BDUs. That should have been easy, given the allotted time. However, that was not the case, as the testers mixed in a slow jogging pace with long sprints up hills, all while having to stay in formation. 200 soldiers running up and down hills at a continuous super-slow to very fast pace created a long snake effect. There were frequent gaps in the formation, with soldiers at the end of the formation lagging behind the main body. Soldiers would trip over others as they tried to catch up to the main body or stay in the formation. An additional challenge was the combat water swim test which required jumping off a ten-foot diving board into the deep end, retrieving your weapon from the side of the pool, and then swimming the length of the pool with the gear – all without touching the bottom. I'm not sure how they disqualified soldiers in this event, but they did.

Similar to the run, there was a required twelve-mile forced march or slow jog which was to be completed in four hours. Again, this task should have been easy, but for the seventy-five pounds of additional gear we had to carry. Furthermore, a few of the unfortunate also had to carry either a heavy radio, or the M60 Machine Gun. In our platoon a recent Navy Seal BUDS graduate who was clearly in great shape carried one of our M60 machine guns and was smoked by the end of the march from carrying the additional twenty-three pounds.

The night land navigation course simply required finding five different orange and white colored coffee cans located about one mile apart from each other in the dense forest, while using only your compass and map. A flashlight with a red lens was the only other tool allowed in this task. The flashlight did illuminate the map, but it wasn't helpful in finding a small coffee can attached to the top of a pole in the middle of the forest. There was a time standard for this course, too, along with being a couple of degrees off on your compass, so many soldiers missed their points or cans and failed the test. Some of those who failed had lost their focus on the task at hand,

PLAN

and a few had lost concentration with worrying about the packs of wild boars that roamed the woods.

Mentally, you had to function through all these evaluations with a sleep-deprived body. You also had to be comfortable walking thirty feet across a twelve-inch board that was twenty-feet up in the air with no safety harness or guard rail. You had to be comfortable sleeping in the mud with snakes and spiders.

To help us survive these tests, the Army taught acronyms so that we could easily remember a key point at the spur of the moment or while under emotional duress, and many of these acronyms proved useful to me in civilian life. "KISS" refers to Keep It Simple Stupid; this concept produced not only outstanding and time-efficient results in the military but also in business and athletics. I recently read about the founder of Jimmy Johns and how he started what has become one of the most successful chains of restaurants in the United States. The founder's father had served in the Army and agreed to loan his son $25,000 to start the business, but if he wasn't successful within 12 months, the son/founder would enlist in the Army. Per the story, the father's only advice to his son was "Keep It Simple." Today, thirty years later, Jimmy John's has over

ANOTHER BATTLE TO WIN

2000 locations and is regarded as one of the most profitable American restaurant chains. It follows a simple business model while providing a menu that customers crave. The Army's acronym has proved useful in the business world.

"PACE" means always having four plans: primary, alternate, contingency, and emergency. Your primary plan often changes almost immediately after the start of a mission or action. Thus, with PACE in mind, you know you have other plans to implement and adapt to the current situation. "A good plan today is better than the perfect plan tomorrow" suggests the reality that a perfect plan is unlikely. The "Seven P Principle" stands for Proper Prior Planning Prevents Piss Poor Performance and is a great reference to the obvious. "GOTWA" is an acronym that requires others to communicate where they are going, others that are going along, the time they will be back, what actions to be taken if they don't come back, and what actions they, themselves, will take if a problem arises. This acronym turned out to be great to use in civilian life for keeping track of your kids or friends. AARs or After-Action Reviews were like breathing in the military, but almost nonexistent in the corporate world. After every military operation, everyone involved from the Colonel at the top to

PLAN

the youngest private would gather and talk about the mission or action we had just completed. We would all go over in detail what we did well, what we needed to improve, and the best way to correct those deficiencies. Later in the corporate world, I experienced how these reviews would only occasionally be conducted. In addition, only a few of the managers would participate and they would not include everyone who had experienced the event. This consistently produced a lack of buy in or acceptance from the workforce and rarely produced the desired effect.

Picture for a moment the CEO of a major corporation asking you how they could do a better job. The few times I participated in a corporate related AAR was almost always when I traveled with the CEO or CFO of a company that we followed to meet with our institutional clients (mutual funds, investment advisors or hedge funds). Between meetings I would brief the management team on what to expect at the next client and ask if they had any questions. Every once in a while, I would be surprised when the CEO or CFO would ask how I thought they did in the prior meeting, how they could change or improve their presentation and what they did well and should continue to do. These leaders of major companies were conducting their own AAR. I would always ask if they had spent time in the military and almost everyone responded that they or a parent had served. Furthermore, regardless of the company's size or the industry in which they competed, their companies almost always had among the best financial returns and stock performance versus their peers. These humble and inquisitive CEOs had learned the importance of an AAR.

Everyone who attended Ranger School had prepared in advance and knew what to expect. Still, the way the Army administered each test by adding elements of stress made each challenge more difficult. Roughly twenty percent of these well-prepared students were gone by the end of the first week, having failed one test or another. A few had become injured and would try the course again once they healed. A few just hadn't really wanted to attend this course, but had been highly encouraged by their leadership. Failing one of these many evaluations allowed them to return to their unit and avoid the pain of the next sixty days. The majority of those who failed this first phase, however, were simply not physically ready or capable or lacked the intestinal fortitude needed to complete the remainder of the course.

PLAN

Over the next two months our class size would dwindle further as we trained and were evaluated in the next three phases. During each of these phases you needed to successfully pass an evaluated leadership position in a simulated military operation and you couldn't be ranked at the bottom of your squad or small unit of peers. You couldn't have committed a major infraction, such as misplacing a weapon or losing contact with a soldier during training. And you had to complete that phase of the course without injury. The extent of any injury would determine whether you were advanced to the next phase, recycled, or returned to your unit. Nevertheless, if you met all criteria, you would be given a "go" to proceed to the next phase.

Those who failed their leadership positions in a specific phase would be afforded a second opportunity where, if successful, they would proceed to the next phase. However, if they failed in this second leadership role, then they would be recycled and remain at that phase, though they could try again with the following class. Those who were "peered" would proceed to the next phase, and if they were ranked poorly in the next phase, they would be dropped from the course and return to their unit.

Upon completion of our seventy-three days of training and evaluation, just 50% of our starting class would be awarded the Ranger Tab.

There were many reasons why soldiers fell short in Ranger School. For some, it was not putting in the daily effort. Others failed because they lacked a detailed plan and the appropriate preparation before they started the course. Another reason some failed is that they didn't adjust their plan throughout the course, itself. Arriving to Ranger School well-prepared was paramount, but given the nature of the course, adjusting one's plan and actions during the training resulted in many successfully graduating when they otherwise might have failed.

Failing a leadership position was gut wrenching; however, a soldier had several days in each phase to prepare for the next leadership role. In addition, those who were ranked poorly by their peers had ample time to correct their behavior and ultimately succeed. Leadership involved many skills, but one of them was the capacity to adjust.

I had months to get ready for the military before I ever reported for day one of training. I used that time to execute a plan that would prepare me for accomplishing my goal of

PLAN

becoming a Ranger. First, I talked to everyone I knew who had knowledge of the Army or military. I was a sponge for each person's suggestions on how to prepare and succeed in my upcoming endeavor. To gain more current and firsthand insight, I had my recruiter arrange a meeting with active duty Ranger-qualified airborne infantry soldiers. I drove from Atlanta to Ft. Bragg, North Carolina and met several active duty soldiers to learn as much as I could on what to expect. These actions and the information gleaned from subject-matter experts was the foundation of my plan.

In order to learn the formal skills and knowledge I would need to successfully complete infantry training and ultimately Ranger School, I read the Army basic training manual and "Ranger Handbook" multiple times. This background would shorten my learning curve and mentally prepared me for the most challenging of tasks that I would face.

So that I was physically prepared, I worked out twice a day, six days a week for months with varying exercises to simulate what I would experience in the military. Nearly every day I jogged with a weighted-down ruck sack and took long runs at a fast pace. I went to the nearby high school and ran stadium steps, mixed with running the track for speed work.

ANOTHER BATTLE TO WIN

To practice mental discipline, I ran twenty quarter-mile circles in our neighborhood to learn how to push myself through pain and monotony. My routine included doing hundreds of push-ups, sit ups, and pull ups. In addition, I went to a firing range where a prior service Marine taught me how to shoot a pistol and rifle. I practiced for hours until I become proficient with firearms. That included not only how to shoot accurately, but also how to disassemble and reassemble these weapons. Taking these actions aided me in weapons qualification during my infantry training.

A great example of planning in a non-military context was our son Alex's preparation for his senior year hockey season. At the end of his junior year of high school, he set a goal to enter his senior year in peak physical condition, bulked up with minimal body fat and with great cardio endurance. He researched the work out regimens and talked with several trainers on what they regarded as the best program. This program would be one that he needed to do daily: what his food and calorie intake should be, what cardio regimen to improve endurance, how to bulk up and gain strength with weight lifting and core workouts. He evaluated several options and developed a couple of plans which he discussed with

PLAN

friends and the trainers, and then chose one that he would follow. Over the course of nine months he diligently followed his plan and consistently made any necessary adjustments. By the start of his senior year hockey season he had gained 30 pounds of pure muscle and he had better endurance. With good planning and dedication to his plan, Alex was able to achieve his goal.

The military was a perfect environment to learn the importance of planning as well as several techniques you could incorporate to improve the odds of accomplishing one's goals.

Use the acronyms (KISS, PACE and AAR) to help guide you in the planning process. They are applicable to non-military situations and increase your odds of success.

Focus on what you hope to accomplish (your intent). The military uses the commander's intent (what they want you to accomplish) and mission statement as the central theme of almost every plan. The mission statement has a specified task (survive cancer, build a business or get a job) and purpose (to live or achieve financial freedom). When in a leadership role

ANOTHER BATTLE TO WIN

relay these to your team and always seek out from your superiors if they are not given.

The Army reinforced the importance of course of action development as a critical component in developing a good plan. You can use this as a foundation for your plan.

First, evaluate your situation and what you must do to succeed.

Talk to others for their opinions, and you will almost always hear at least one great idea that you might otherwise have missed. Consider all the variables that can impact your plan. These are not inclusive or even appropriate for most challenges a person might plan for, but as an example in the military they would include the terrain, weather, moon illumination, enemy situation, friendly forces in your vicinity, rules of engagement, time line, mission statement, commander's intent, scheme of maneuver, rally points, and medical support, just to name a few. In the corporate world they could include product or service, competitive advantage, competition, pricing, advertising, marketing, market share, manufacturing efficiencies, margins, return on investment, free cash flow, economic cycles, logistics, human resources, regulation, compensation, and stakeholders to name a few.

PLAN

Write a couple of different plans (remember PACE as some could be your alternate or contingency plans), and go over them with someone you respect to determine which is the best option.

Then finalize and put your plan into action.

Constantly evaluate the results for improvement (AAR), and tweak as needed to make the plan even better.

Hope is never a plan. Dreams or hopes on their own will not result in success. You need to have definitive goals and a detailed plan with the specific dates that you expect to accomplish each task or phase.

You will always have to work hard and push yourself daily to stay on course.

These collective actions will have a positive impact and take you one step closer to achieving your goal.

FOUR

Live in the Now

Army OCS

How does anyone prepare for six months of cancer treatment with so many unknowns? Nobody is ever ready for it. To be fair, though, being treated for cancer isn't all up to you. The medical protocol has its own inner life, its own timing and standards that have to be met whether the patient

LIVE IN THE NOW

is ready or not. Still, each patient has some past experience of difficulty to draw from and some past experience solving problems to use as a guideline for facing the challenges of chemo and radiation. In that way, I was no different from many others facing cancer treatment. But I had the advantage of working through an extremely challenging time in the military, and I got some of my fortitude from the years I spent there. I got at least one of my principles for living there. My ultimate success in beating cancer came from the same way I attacked Army OCS. That experience was four months of a daily living hell where you had to continually push yourself. I learned how important it is to focus on only one day at a time. The principle of "Live in the now!" served me well then and later.

Day one of OCS started with 125 active duty soldiers who all wanted to become officers standing in formation with our "A bags" or duffel bags filled with clothing and personal items. We were then taken upstairs to our two-person rooms, told to leave the padlocked "A bags" on a bunk, and return downstairs to formation. Next began the start of what I called the "uniform clown game." We had a specific amount of time to run upstairs, change into a silly uniform, run back downstairs, and be in a standard military formation. One of the many strange combinations we heard that day was "Army dress top, brown T-shirt, BDU bottom, left foot combat boot and black sock, right foot flip flop, and black watch cap. You have 10 minutes. Go." Once we got to our room, we had to first unlock our "A Bags", and then dump all the neatly packed contents on our bunks or the floor just to find the requested clothing. The first several times, only a few of the candidates made it back to formation in the allotted time. Upon each failure the instructors punished us with pushups and flutter kicks. As the hours stretched on, more of us started making it downstairs to formation in the allotted time and dressed as the instructors had ordered. They would then complicate even further the mismatched uniforms they wanted us to wear, or shorten the time standard. We played this game over and over for hours. We must have looked like a herd of sweaty clowns, continually gasping for air. I made it through by keeping my head down and concentrating on the task ahead.

Around 2300 hours or eleven PM, we were told day one had ended; we should prepare for lights out and expect an 0530 wake up call. The next morning would be our first APFT. At this point we were all ready for the day to be done.

LIVE IN THE NOW

We looked forward to getting some sleep so our bodies would be ready for the next day. Just before lights out, though, one of the instructors said that someone had committed an infraction, and for the next hour we were once again punished with pushups and flutter kicks. The instructor was not satisfied with the punishment and decided that we needed to duck walk around the hallways until midnight. We went to bed tired and sore only to be woken up three hours later, at 0300 or three AM, to the pounding sound of banging metal trash cans.

Shortly thereafter, we took our first APFT in one of the many Georgia thunder and lightning storms. The pounding rain had little impact on the sit up and push up portion of the test, but the howling wind created a serious headwind we had to run into half the time on the half-mile track. A large percentage of the candidates did not pass their first APFT. The weather had some impact, but the previous day's non-stop instructor-led smoke sessions plus sleep deprivation had done their intended job of ensuring most would fail. We had been in this course less than twenty-four hours and were soon to find out that the pain only got worse and never stopped. Just making it to each morning's wakeup call would become a victory for most. This experience would grind into my one-day-at-a-time mission, but I didn't lose my focus. I, along with many other officer candidates pushed ourselves daily and focused only on the now.

Roughly two months later, we were still enduring this daily grind without a single day of relief. We were on the last of five days spent in the field conducting non-stop day and night land navigation. All were happy to be away from the barracks, classrooms, and so many sets of watchful eyes. The instructors were masters in consistently finding fault for the smallest infraction. As a result, we were physically punished, sleep deprived, and constantly tested on our ability to suck up another painful day without quitting.

The instructors had been in a gnarly mood since the second day of land navigation, which began with an impromptu formation early that morning. One of the instructors standing before us held up a condom and asked, "whose is this?" In formation you never got to see facial expressions of others, but snickers rumbled through the group. Most were thinking, but not expressing, the same thought: *Who in this group had the guts to have sex during OCS?* We were a mixed class of male and female candidates, and apparently two months with no sex had been too much for two of our candidates. Many of us were suspicious, wary that the instructors were playing another mind game and had fabricated this unique story. The instructor then pointed to the right side of our formation and said, "We found this still warm condom over there in the bushes, behind the big trees." This time in unison we all looked in that direction with our minds now racing on who it might be. Would the guilty parties fess up, only to be kicked out of the course? The instructors yelled, threatened, and smoked us in their attempt to identify the guilty couple, which was never ascertained. Given the large number of non-married soldiers in our class, most of us believed that this story being told of a hook up in the woods had actually occurred. That said, most of us were not only surprised at the audacity of this brave yet risky act, but that the evidence had not been buried.

The intensity of the physical challenges never let up. The land navigation training was conducted in the wintertime, which at Ft. Benning meant temperatures hovering north of freezing. The terrain in the area was a thick pine forest set on a series of slightly rolling hills. There were some upsides to training in the winter. There wasn't the normally thick undergrowth of vegetation which slowed your movement

ANOTHER BATTLE TO WIN

through the woods. The cold also meant no snakes, which always caused some to worry during the night course. Still, the challenges were hard. The instructors would give us five, eight-digit coordinates, which we would then plot on a map. We had four hours using only a compass and map to locate five coffee-sized cans, each about one mile apart and deep in the woods. The night sessions were even more challenging. Since we didn't use flashlights, getting smacked in the face with branches or tripping over fallen timber was the norm.

By day five, everyone was tired, our legs sore from multiple days of continuous walking up and down hills. Many had massive blisters on their feet, and all were cold to the core. The training would end when the last of the candidates completed their night course and made it back to our camp. Those of us who had already completed the night course were warming ourselves around burn barrels, or fifty-five-gallon drums filled with fire. We were all ready to be back in our barracks, taking a warm shower, going to bed, and getting more sleep than we had been allowed in the field. At that moment many lapsed in their judgement, forgetting that these cold woods and our sore feet were actually substantially better than being back in our barracks with the endless mind games and smoke sessions.

When the last candidate rolled into camp, the instructors put us in formation to break some unexpected news. "As you can see, we had a mix up in our transportation request and only have one truck, so the majority of you are going to have hump, or hike, the 15 miles back to the barracks. If you are hurting and think you can't make it, jump on the truck now." Every one of us was hurting in some form. Many of us wondered if this was just another game to see who was going to put their head down or who would focus on the now and forge on? Who was actually going to get on the one truck and potentially be labeled a quitter? Around fifteen of the ninety candidates walked over and got on the truck, while the rest of us started walking. Forty-five minutes later we were out of the woods, and on hardball, or the pavement of the closest road. There stood the truck with the candidates who had recently given up, plus four empty trucks. Another mind game played, with the instructors humiliating those who had taken the easy way out, several of which would never graduate.

These were just two of the one hundred plus very similar days I experienced during OCS. Every day we had intense physical training or thrashings of pushups, little sleep, and too much to do with not enough time. We started with 125 well-screened and selected soldiers. At the end of the course, only 68 were commissioned. The mindset of those who graduated was that regardless of their daily suffering, nothing would stop them from their goal of being commissioned an officer. They all worked hard, sucked up the daily pain, and put in their maximum effort every waking moment.

Twelve months after being commissioned, I had successfully completed five different infantry schools, such as Pathfinder and Ranger School. I had been in the Army for almost two years. If you counted every day that I saw Susie and newborn baby, including weekends, it was ninety days. At some point several of us calculated that given our long hours of training or deployment, we were barely making the minimum wage. That was if you were an officer. Some studies showed that the majority of the married enlisted soldiers below the rank of E5, or sergeant, qualified under the official threshold of poverty.

Some of the soldiers would occasionally engage in challenges or dares to pass the time and potentially help an enlisted soldier's cash flow, should they win. One of the more

LIVE IN THE NOW

memorable bets I witnessed occurred during a training exercise's chow break in the Georgia woods. Every MRE, or meal ready to eat, comes with a small bottle of tabasco sauce, but some soldiers carried their favorite sauce in their rucksack. A couple of the soldiers were discussing whether it was possible to chug an entire bottle of hot sauce without throwing up. After several minutes of the soldiers bantering back and forth on the subject, a bet was set. Sergeant Smith volunteered to drink an eight-ounce bottle of super-hot tabasco sauce within two minutes and then refrain from throwing up for the following ten minutes. If he was successful, the other soldiers would pay him fifty dollars. Should he not win the bet, he didn't owe them anything other than his own personal pain and pride.

He easily chugged the eight-ounce of hot juice within the two minutes and then sat back, waiting to see if he could win. The soldiers who would be paying off the bet if he was successful did their best imitations of hurling to aid their side of the bet. Sergeant Smith sat stoically but soon had foaming saliva oozing out of both corners of his mouth. Private First Class Stowling, who was solely a spectator, was the first to hurl only a few feet away from Sergeant Smith, just from watching this episode unfold. That action caused Sergeant Smith to buckle and appear to be in the process of following Private First Class Stowling's lead, but he didn't. One second after the ten minutes was called, Sergeant Smith leaned to his left, simultaneously tossing his now red-colored lunch while also extending his arm with a hand open to collect his 50 dollars.

Sergeant Smith had evaluated his options and knew the price he had to pay to succeed. He physically suffered for a short period of time to gain an economic advantage, which in this case was almost a full day of his after-tax pay. He was willing to pay the price to help his economic situation. He knew how to focus only on the now and push himself through extreme discomfort.

Another example of pushing yourself to an extreme, was my son Drew during a high school hockey play-off game. His line (Drew and two teammates) had just come off the ice and were sitting on the bench awaiting their next shift. Drew took off his glove to make a quick equipment adjustment, while at that exact moment two of his teammates on defense were ending their shift and jumping over the boards. A razor-sharp skate from one of them tore into his right middle finger,

LIVE IN THE NOW

ripping flesh to the bone. A local doctor put in six-eight stiches and reminded him of the quote from the movie *The Replacements."* "Chicks dig scars, pain goes away but glory lasts forever." Then the doctor said, "Now forget the pain and go get some glory". Drew was back on the ice to start the third and final period with his stick holding hand throbbing and the pain progressively getting worse. His team was down by one, and during his third shift of that period, Drew scored the game- tying goal. He had lived in the now.

A close to home example of just living in the now occurred prior to my surgery and the start of the chemo treatment. Susie, was a wet noodle of emotions given the unknown, especially whether I would be alive in the coming months. She became paralyzed by the scary thoughts running through her mind. We talked at length on the process of living in the now and focusing only on one day at a time. She adopted the mindset which helped her navigate months of uncertainty. She learned to not think about the future and the varying what-ifs; instead, she focused only on what she needed to accomplish each day. Many friends and family remarked how well she was able to cope considering the circumstances.

ANOTHER BATTLE TO WIN

At times the pain, fear or stress will be extreme, and this current obstacle is just one of several that you are facing in close succession. How do you successfully battle the current obstacle knowing hours or even minutes later the next challenge is even greater? During these periods you focus only on the current moment and mentally block out what lies ahead. SGT Smith's success was because he focused only on the present and not one minute in the future. During my cancer treatment when I had extreme nausea and was exercising, I only focused on walking the hallways as fast as possible without hitting a caregiver. I would not think about the dual procedures of lung puncture and spinal tap with their bolts of pain that awaited me in the hours ahead.

Goals, dreams, and detailed plans are not enough to succeed. You have to work hard and push yourself every day to make your plan happen.

You will probably have to endure pain or hardship. But short-term suffering will take you one step closer to achieving long term success.

LIVE IN THE NOW

When faced with tough mental or physical challenges, you can't ever quit. It's ok not to do some difficult things a second time, but you do need to finish whatever you've started.

There are some strategies that can help you carry on to the end. The main one is simple. During the tough periods, focus on only one day at a time. When the pain is extreme and the current obstacle is only one of several you will confront, focus only on the moment and mentally block out your next challenge. "Live in the now!" I lived by this principle in OCS, Ranger School, during long deployments, at times in the corporate world, and I lived by it during my cancer treatment. I believe in it. It has helped me survive

FIVE

Learn

Lt. David

Today, you can find an answer to any question or a solution to almost any problem within seconds. That doesn't mean this short cut to learning on the internet is the right answer or the best solution. My prognosis per the cancer experts on the internet had me long ago buried six feet under

LEARN

in a flag-draped coffin. Today, many individuals rely more on the quick answer or solution. They spend less time reading, interacting, and asking questions of others than they should. Being a sponge for knowledge and continuous learning are keys to success. There is no short cut, and those who are successful rarely slow down their drive to learn more.

Lt. David spent a couple of years in college before enlisting in the Army. He served in the 1st Ranger Battalion, where he successfully completed Ranger School and became an NCO or non-commissioned officer. After serving several years with the Rangers, he wanted a transfer to Special Forces. He passed SFAS or Special Forces Assessment and Selection, and then the Q Course which earned him his Special Forces Tab and a place on one of the teams. Lt. David was assigned to 10th Group, where he ultimately became a senior NCO, E-7, Sergeant First Class, and served for years. Along the way he went through Delta Force selection and supposedly came close to being one of the rumored three out of the 100+ high-speed infantry studs who were ultimately selected.

My first interaction with Lt. David was the third day of Army OCS when he was at the front of our 5:30 PT formation. He had the highest score on the APFT the day prior and would lead our daily PT warm ups until someone scored higher. I still remember his opening comments just prior to beginning of our first exercise: "Beyond SERE School (Survive Evade Resist and Escape), Scuba School was the hardest physical event I have ever done. The first exercise we did at Scuba School on day one was "flutter kicks." We will do the same number that I did in Scuba School, which was 200 four-count kicks." Flutter kicks is an intense abdominal exercise. Few are capable of continuing the exercise for more than three to four minutes without a break. Over the next ten minutes there were numerous grunts and moans from our group, with only a few able to complete the exercise. All the while doing flutter kicks, himself, Lt. David was calling cadence or voice commands during the entire exercise, which made the exercise even more difficult, and he did not even break into a sweat. He was in excellent shape and just as clearly a soldier with strong self-discipline.

Our OCS class was only for active duty soldiers and filled with dozens of highly talented NCOs and warrant officers who each had many years of experience. Lt. David at this point had over ten years of military experience and ended up being our class honor graduate. Then at IOBC or Infantry Officers Basic

LEARN

Course, after six months of training and evaluation, he was selected the honor graduate of our class of 150 infantry second lieutenants. I would go on to learn a lot from him.

When I arrived at the 24th Infantry Division, I was assigned to the same company as Lt. David, and we spent the next year as fellow platoon leaders. During our two years of serving together, he demonstrated time and again that he was not only a PT stud, but technically and tactically a military genius. He read every key military book and army manual more than once. He knew the solution to every problematic situation but would still seek out and listen to each person's opinion and recommendation. His grasp of military tactics, enemy doctrine, and Army regulations was light years ahead of his peers. He was more knowledgeable than our commanders. Later, he would transfer and serve as a platoon leader at 1st Ranger Battalion. There he was referred to as a "man child among studs."

Though Lt. David was in the one-tenth of one percent of an already highly competitive field, he always assumed he didn't know the answer, even when he usually had the best solution. He always sought others' opinions to see what he might be missing, and most important of all, he never stopped learning.

Lt. David was the epitome of a true sponge, in addition to being one of the humblest men you would ever meet.

Mitch

Another example to reinforce the importance of continual learning is that of Mitch. As a junior in high school, Mitch was rated as one of the top one hundred high school baseball players in the United States. He spent his youth pursuing a dream of playing in the Major Leagues. That meant he would practice for hours every day and forgo vacations in lieu of a baseball camp or more time spent at the batting cages. Adhering to his plan, working hard each day through adversity; continually learning all that he could enabled him to reach the top of the top of his elite peer group.

I first met Mitch in 2008. He was a senior at a prestigious university where he was a four-year starter on their baseball team, having accepted their Division One scholarship. My firm's equity sales department at the time had never hired an undergraduate who hadn't worked somewhere else for a couple of years after graduating from college. One of our

LEARN

salespeople on the New York team had played baseball at Vanderbilt, and due to this baseball connection, brought Mitch into the office to meet with several of his team's salespeople. Mitch was quiet and listened more than he talked. In addition, his below 3.5 GPA did not impress some of the members of the New York team, so they passed on hiring him.

About two to three months after Mitch's visit with the New York team, the Midwest team was interviewing to fill a junior sales position. The majority of our hires throughout the years had been graduating MBA students from highly ranked schools. The Vanderbilt salesman suggested that we should consider Mitch as a candidate for the team. When Mitch interviewed, his knowledge of the industry, the role we fulfilled, and what it took to be successful was extensive. Given the interest in equity sales, we had dozens of potential candidates for consideration. And as a team we did not place the same emphasis on the candidate's GPA as others in our department, including management. Our view was that Mitch was not only attending a challenging school but playing Division One baseball at the same time. That, in our opinion, was equivalent to someone working full time while attending a very demanding school.

ANOTHER BATTLE TO WIN

To the chagrin of some, we hired Mitch, and he became the first undergraduate our department hired directly out of school for a position in sales. He spent the next several years practicing FILO, or first in and last out, which showed all on our floor that he had a dedicated and focused approach to work. He developed a broad and diverse base of mentors, using their knowledge to help him build client relationships, and he worked to learn our product faster and better than most. Mitch spent four-years studying and passing both the CFA or Chartered Financial Analyst and CMT or Certified Market Technician, while working full-time. Getting the CFA was normal for our employees who analyzed companies and managed equity portfolios. But only a few of our thousands would have both the CFA and CMT. It was exceptionally rare to see a salesperson working at a Wall Street sell-side research shop, such as our firm, have both designations.

In a highly competitive field, coupled with a firm that was filled with enormous talent, Mitch grew to be ranked in the top quartile of his counterparts within a few years. His peer group on average was also fifteen years older than he. He never stopped learning and was the same dedicated student of the equity markets and equity sales as he had been of baseball.

LEARN

Roughly seven years after Mitch started his career in equity sales, he was chosen to co-manage a 500 million-dollar equity fund. Mitch succeeded in becoming the one-percent of those in the industry who become portfolio managers and manage money professionally. He also accomplished that at least one decade, if not two, earlier than his portfolio manager peers.

Mitch displayed a thirst for continuous learning. Regardless of how much he knew, he always assumed there was more to learn.

Luck is simply the result of extensive preparation, practice, and persistence. Mitch would acknowledge that he benefited from a touch of luck considering the Midwest team's willingness to hire an undergraduate with no experience, but he made his further luck by learning how to be the best.

Favorite Stock

One of my best and most humbling learning experiences happened in 2009. At the time I had over ten years, or 30,000 hours, of experience analyzing stocks. A new teammate just out of business school pitched me a great stock story, which I researched in depth. First, I talked to our analyst regarding the company. He was regarded as one of the best analysts on Wall Street in this particular sector, and he was a fan of the company. Subsequently an institutional client of mine pitched me this same story, relaying that his firm was one of the company's largest shareholders. He told me every detail that he was legally allowed to share, which was substantially more than our analyst knew. Finally, I traveled with the CEO of a competitor of this company, and he not only knew a great deal about the company but was close to their management team. He shared in great specifics all that he was allowed to disclose. Tying together this disparate information, I then knew more about this company than anyone except its senior management. In addition, I had tens of thousands of hours of equity analysis experience. I had been the sponge, assumed I knew little, and was curious in all regards to learn even more each day regarding this company.

Early in this process, before I knew a fraction of what I ultimately learned, I had bought and sold a small position in this company's stock to become more acquainted with their trading dynamics. I made a quick twenty-percent profit. Now, with this confluence of sources all confirming the stock was a

LEARN

great opportunity, I bought a much larger position than normal in the company. I proceeded to lose all my profit in addition to a taking a substantial overall loss. Even with all that information and experience, I had been dead wrong. I totally missed the true sentiment or trading psychology around the stock. As I painfully learned, regardless of all your knowledge, or expertise, you can and will fail. But there is still a learning goal to be reached. I used this experience as another lesson learned and proceeded to incorporate that into my future stock trades. Negative experiences provide some of your best lessons learned and contribute the most to your overall growth and development.

Today with the internet we all have so many easy short cuts, and many assume they can find the quick answer. But real learning isn't always quick or easy, and no matter what you know or think you know, there is always a lot you don't know. There are always others who know more, are better prepared, trained, practiced or qualified. Those who are supposedly the best or have succeeded have continued to learn, and that commitment to learning is responsible for their extraordinary success.

ANOTHER BATTLE TO WIN

We are all unique and our aspirations vary, thus there is no perfect path to follow or single person to emulate. But there are common actions used by those who have succeeded, and you can use as a guide on your quest to learn.

Regardless of where you are in your journey always be a sponge for more knowledge and experience. Whenever you think you have a great answer, plan, or solution – remember Lt. David and Mitch. They were both in the top $1/10^{th}$ of 1%, yet still they were sponges, always asking questions and assuming there was more to learn. Emulate their mindset, always be curious and push yourself to learn.

In addition, become an avid reader. Seek out the experts as their years of experience are condensed into a few hours of reading. Their lessons learned can be your blueprint for success. Read several books and articles from different authors regarding the same subject and aggregate their unique lessons into a single collective thought process and plan. A plethora of great books can provide you a base of knowledge and form a solid foundation for your own life plan. A few of those to read are: *Make Your Bed* by William McRaven, *Seven*

LEARN

Habits of Highly Successful People by Steven Covey, *Think and Grow Rich* by Napoleon Hill and *How to Win Friends and Influence People* by Dale Carnegie. Each of these books or their experts have been read by millions and are worthy of being studied extensively.

Finally think AAA in your learning process: Take **A**ction, Conduct **A**fter-Action Reviews, and **A**djust your plan. Taking action is the hardest for many as it entails changing your routine and allocating the time each day to learn, but taking action can become commonplace after several weeks if you do the right things. Spend less time on video games or watching TV. Simply turning off your phone will give you ample time to direct toward gaining knowledge. This self-directed learning time can be funneled towards reading, practicing to improve a weakness, rehearsing an upcoming action, or just improving your plan.

Conduct an After-Action Review after every action in which you participate, and include every person who was involved. It can be an extensive review or as brief as taking a minute to mentally replay your actions. Learn from what you did well and need to repeat or incorporate into your plan.

ANOTHER BATTLE TO WIN

Moreover, learn from those actions what you need to improve and how that will be accomplished.

Adjust your plan after each AAR or when conditions change and warrant a new direction. This process is continuous as you are constantly learning from all sources and adapting your plan from your lessons learned.

Never stop learning. Be a sponge. Be curious. Search out and listen to mentors, and ask questions. Assume you don't know the answer even when you think you do.

SIX

Expect the Unexpected

Mr. Bread

Anything that can go wrong will go wrong is "Murphy's Law." During most military training exercises, especially Basic Training and Ranger School, I saw Murphy's observation multiple times a day, every day. Preparing ourselves to expect the unexpected was a daily challenge given the ever-changing situations – especially when we didn't even know what we didn't know.

Basic Training had each minute of every day planned in detail, and all with a specific training or learning purpose. The drill sergeants were masters in playing mind games to reinforce the lessons that they wanted us never to forget. Eating meals in the DFAC or dining facility, nicknamed the chow hall, was one of the only times of the day when we had some sanctuary from their endless games. But there were rules in the chow hall like everywhere else. In the DFAC, you only took what the servers put on your plate or you were allowed to take, which meant no desserts, extras, or seconds.

The drill sergeant's table was strategically placed just beyond the serving line and near the entrance to the main dining room. One day early in Basic Training, one of the privates took an extra piece of bread, which he hid under his plate. As he was walking into the dining room, one of the drill sergeants had him stop and asked why his plate was elevated slightly above his tray. He froze, assumed a deer in the headlight's stare, and panicked, unable to get any words out of his mouth. The sergeant ordered him to pick up his plate,

EXPECT THE UNEXPECTED

revealing the hidden but now mushed piece of bread. The drill sergeant simply said, "Private, put that extra, non-allowed piece of bread in your right cargo pocket. Don't wash those BDUs or touch that bread until I tell you."

Every morning after PT or Physical Training, showers, and barracks inspection, our company of 150 privates would fall into formation. We would then march to the DFAC, eat, and start our day of training. For the next several days following the extra bread incident, during this morning formation we all witnessed the same event. The drill sergeant who had caught the private taking the extra piece of mushy bread would yell out, "Private Bread, front and center: show me Mr. Bread" After a quick examination of the bread, the drill sergeant would command the private to put the bread back in his cargo pocket. By the tenth day, the bread had become a ball of black moldy crumbs. The drill sergeant simply said, "Private, you can now eat the bread."

It was a memorable lesson for all of us to follow the rules, expect the unexpected, and be prepared for the consequences if we didn't.

The vast majority of infantry soldiers either smoked, dipped snuff, or chewed tobacco to curb their appetite and help them stay awake when they were sleep deprived, which was every day. Ranger School allowed you to use tobacco at will in the field, but during each phase's train-up and cadre-led instructions, permission for tobacco use was required and rarely given. Dozing off in class or getting caught sleeping resulted in a "major minus" chit. Receiving two "major minus" chits in any of the four phases of training translated to failure and soldier would have to repeat that phase.

During class one day after several days of little sleep, several of us were using snuff without permission in an attempt to not doze off. Halfway through the class, the instructor said, "Kneisel, do you have a dip in?" My quick reply was, "Yes, sergeant." He simply said, "Swallow it now or suffer the consequences." I clearly had not learned the lesson from "Mr. Bread" and proceeded to swallow the dip, almost threw up, and would never break that rule again.

Ranger School, The Desert

Roughly eighteen months after my start of Army Basic Training, I began day one of Ranger School. When I attended in 1993, the course was seventy-three days long and had four phases. These four phases included the indoctrination or weed out phase at Ft. Benning, followed by the desert, mountains, and swamp phases. Almost everyone who went through Ranger School was in great shape and had already passed their own unit's pre-ranger program, which was usually two weeks long. The students were mainly from one of the ten Army infantry divisions, but they also came from the Marines, Navy Seals, Air Force Para Rescue, and non-U.S. allied militaries. A British Royal Marine officer and a Navy Seal were in my platoon.

The course was known for being one of the best leadership schools in the military and also for having a high recycle or fail rate. Even though everyone came prepared, only fifty-percent of our class would graduate without being recycled or forced to redo at least one of the phases. On average over the two-month-plus course, we ate two meals and had less than four hours sleep a day. Injuries were common, and we were checked daily by medics to prevent us from hiding one. Many of the injuries, such as cellulitis, could become deadly if gone untreated, but injury also meant recycling for the student.

They told us that by the end of the course we would have the immune system of an AIDS patient.

The desert phase, which is no longer part of the course, was conducted about twenty miles outside of El Paso, Texas. During our indoctrination to this phase, we were briefed on such issues as the presence of rattle snakes, and that it only rained about seven days a year in the area. During our actual time spent in the desert, our class was soaked and chilled to the bone for four of those seven days a year that they normally received rainfall. These were long-lasting torrential thunderstorms. The weather created a more difficult environment for all, especially those in leadership positions, who were being evaluated.

One night we were executing an attack mission. We staged our rucksacks in a patrol base which was a half-mile from the objective of the mission. We also left two soldiers to stand guard over our gear. Once we completed the mission, which all considered to be one of our rare successes, we conducted our movement back to our patrol base or staging area. When back at the patrol base, most of the students in leadership roles would probably receive a "go," and mentally be on their way to the mountain phase. But completing this desert phase wasn't that simple.

On the movement across the flat desert terrain to our patrol base, we kept stopping for extended periods, and it soon became apparent that we were either lost or couldn't find our two men and rucks. You would think it would be easy to find thirty large rucksacks and the two soldiers, but that was not the case in the desert night where everything looked the same. In this situation, like all others we had conducted, the two soldiers with radios would signal us into our patrol base with either the flashes from their red lensed-covered flashlights, or squelched signals from their radios. But we didn't hear or see either.

After an hour of searching, we finally found our gear, one embarrassed sleeping soldier, but no second soldier. The Ranger evaluators stopped the mission or training exercise and had us in the front leaning rest position, doing push-ups as we yelled out in unison the missing student's name. In the far distance we heard his faint reply. He followed the sound of our yelling, and in short order he found our platoon. He explained that he had gone to take a dump and had gotten lost. He was pulled from training the next morning.

ANOTHER BATTLE TO WIN

Roughly half of our desert phase class, which included many outstanding soldiers, were required to spend an extra month of their life in the desert in order to redo this phase. The Ranger who fell asleep with our rucks on the night attack mission caused that mission's entire chain of command to fail, though the actual mission had been conducted to perfection. The rain and lightning were so severe on one of those rainy nights, that the evaluators took all our weapons and radios as a safety precaution. They then left us alone for several hours until the lightning stopped and the storm passed over. At that point the mission was back on, but many of the Ranger students had fallen asleep and the chain of command could not get them to wake up or function effectively. Most of the student leadership failed this mission.

The desert phase of Ranger School included a series of unexpected events in which we had to react and adapt. Better planning for all contingencies might have mitigated some of those daily disasters, but "Murphy" would also ensure that some inevitably just happened.

Those of us who passed this phase knew that we were lucky. We were moving on to the Mountain Phase that was conducted outside of Dahlonega, Georgia.

EXPECT THE UNEXPECTED

Ranger School, The Mountains

Dahlonega, Georgia is a picturesque and somewhat famous turn of the century mining town, located 60 miles north of Atlanta on the edge of the Smokey Mountains. Tens of thousands of tourists visit each year to see the old mines, pan for gold in the crystal-clear streams, or start or end their hike on the Appalachian Trail which runs from Dahlonega to Maine. The terrain in the area is filled with outstanding scenery, dense vegetation, waterfalls, cliffs, and very steep hills. If we thought we had seen it all in the desert, we found out that the mountains brought its unique challenges, and Murphy's Law was with us every single night.

We spent our preparation time rappelling up and down the mountain cliffs, learning to tie intricate knots for the ropes we would be using, and getting updated on the local hazards that awaited us. We all knew there could be weather issues, given the numerous thunderstorms in Georgia. And there would be pain inflicted on us from humping up, down, and sideways around the mountains while carrying heavy gear. The poisonous snakes would now include the copperhead, and there was even a remote chance of a black bear encounter.

The ropes, knot-tying and rappelling refresher highlighted the risk of walking over cliffs in this terrain, especially if we weren't paying attention to our maps and land navigation. What we didn't know until the briefings was that our missions would be conducted during a lunar cycle that had near zero illumination. Once we were up in the mountains at night, we could touch our hands to our noses and not see our fingers. Even with our NVDs or night vision devices, the tree canopy blocked what little we had of the moon's illumination, and we could only see a few feet. The movements at night would be very challenging and filled with potential peril.

Early in our field problem or series of continuous missions, I was 100% confident that I had passed my leadership position when I had been the weapons squad leader on a convoy ambush. Given the illumination issues, I was breathing a sigh of relief that I had received a day mission and believed that I was a "go" to the swamp phase held near Eglin, AFB in the Florida, Panhandle.

Days later we were told that the upcoming night mission would be a long movement through a clear-cut forest, which

EXPECT THE UNEXPECTED

is an area where the trees have been cut and left to die on the ground. Tactically walking over and around all these downed trees and their branches would be extremely difficult to accomplish in the daylight, but conducting the mission at night would be a huge task and near impossible to perform with no illumination. The prior two nights, the near zero illumination had produced a couple of mishaps. Luckily there were no major injuries. While sliding down a muddy mountain slope, one soldier became entangled with a fallen tree. He then placed his M16 weapon to the side so he could free himself from the branches. After getting untangled from the fallen tree, he couldn't find his M16 in the dark, which was a major error on him and an ultimate "no go" for his chain of command. Another soldier somehow lost his Kevlar helmet, which was supposed to be strapped to his rucksack. It had tumbled down a mountainside, only to be found the next day. Both soldiers were dropped from the course.

We all felt sorry for whoever had leadership positions this third night of near zero illumination, as these soldiers would likely all fail and run the risk of being recycled. Late in the afternoon, one of the instructors started calling out the roster numbers of who was going to be in the night mission's leadership roles, and my number was called. I had clearly been given a no-go on my last mission and was at risk of being recycled. I had forgotten Murphy and been overly confident that I was done with this phase's leadership positions. I had not mentally prepared for this leadership role. Once my heart rate normalized following the anxiety of hearing my roster number called, I quickly thought of all my lessons learned from previous experiences. Mentally I prepared for the mission as I walked over to get instructions from the assigned Ranger walker or evaluator.

This Ranger sergeant had already shadowed me on my last mission, so there was some familiarity that went both ways. He gave me the mission brief with the coordinates to mark the objective and asked what I thought. I said, "Not to be pessimistic, but given the lack of illumination and having to move through clear-cut terrain, we will never make the objective until hours after sunrise. We'll fail to complete the mission in the required time." His reply was simply, "Why don't you hug the logging trails and skirt around the downed timber?" We had all been explicitly told that we could never use or hug any logging trail and would receive a no-go if we tried. I replied, "I didn't know we could. Are you ok with us

EXPECT THE UNEXPECTED

hugging the trail?" He simply said, "Of course. With zero illumination, no one could move the distance we have to travel over and through a downed forest, and make the objective in the allotted time." We completed the mission, and during my out-brief the next morning, my evaluator asked how I thought I did. I told him the logging trail helped a ton, but still thought I hadn't done great. His reply was "I thought you did ok, but I know that you did an outstanding job on your first ambush mission. You should have been given a go then, so you, Ranger, are now a go out of the Mountain Phase."

Two and a half months after starting Ranger School, we were back at Ft. Benning. Roughly 125 of the starting 250 students graduated and earned their Ranger Tab.

Most of us never learn from our experiences, unless we suffer physically, emotionally, or financially. I would learn from all three of those experiences in the military and in business. Swallowing a dip Copenhagen was just one of many and among the least painful of all the unexpected situations where I endured some form of personal suffering. But what I learned was significant:

ANOTHER BATTLE TO WIN

Follow the rules. This will save you a lot of pain.

Remember Murphy's Law of "Anything that can go wrong, will go wrong."

Expect the unexpected and be prepared for the unplanned twists and turns in your life's journey.

Be curious, ask questions and listen intently to everyone's concerns and opinions. This will usually shed some light on risks you may have missed.

Be a devil's advocate and role play what could go wrong and how you will counteract.

Spend as much time as possible in the planning process with attention to detail.

Rehearse with others your plan. Talk through each component or phase searching for what could go wrong and how you will react and take corrective action.

If your plan has gone awry and you are feeling Murphy's pain, mentally conduct a quick course of action analysis. Analyze the situation, develop a new plan, wargame and act.

These collective actions will allow you to avoid, be better prepared and adapt to many of the unexpected pitfalls.

SEVEN

Be Positive

Cancer Treatment

"You can accomplish more with sugar and honey than with a hammer," is what my grandmother would always say. Yes, there are times in life that the hammer is needed, but a positive attitude and kind soul are attributes that will provide untold benefits to you in your journey.

ANOTHER BATTLE TO WIN

During my eight separate week-long visits to the hospital, the importance of a positive attitude, kind soul, and leaving the hammer in the toolbox was reinforced on several occasions. The oncology center at the teaching hospital where I underwent my treatment was located in a brand-new wing with spacious rooms and an outstanding staff of doctors and nurses. As comforting as this new facility could be, there were issues other than my disease to overcome. I asked every doctor I met what I could do to achieve my goal of cancer remission. The resounding answer from each was to stay active each day and always maintain a positive attitude. They told me daily exercise would increase my energy, thus allowing my body to tolerate the drugs, fight infection, and generate a faster recovery between sessions. This, in turn, would allow me to start each of my eight weekly chemo cycles sooner than planned. Given the universal opinion of the doctors regarding the importance of daily exercise, being active was the cornerstone of my plan to accomplish my goal of beating this disease. With that in mind, I knew I needed to get ample sleep each night and be able to eat and nourish my body, even when I was nauseous and felt disgust for any type of food, except for popsicles.

BE POSITIVE

At the same time, the nurses who managed my daily treatment were following their detailed inpatient oncology protocol which entailed checking on me every two hours. My sleep was interrupted so often that I was merely taking a series of naps throughout the night. On my first of forty nights spent in the hospital, I had only a couple hours of sleep and woke the next day tired and in a haze. The drugs were draining; it was a challenge in itself to maintain enough energy each day to workout. I knew that I would need the nurses on my side if I was going to accomplish my plan and goals.

Producing the optimal situation started with Susie bringing treats to my hospital room for the staff. I always had bowls of different candy on display and always encouraged the staff to partake. Those candy bowls were the introduction to my positive relations with the staff. I didn't have a busy schedule in the hospital other than the nurses constantly changing the various chemo-related drugs attached to the semi-permanent PIC IV in my right bicep. So besides focusing on daily exercise, I tried getting to know everyone on the staff. I went out of my way to be kind to everyone and to learn as much as possible about my caregivers during the process. I got to know all the nurses, their assistants, and the people cleaning the room. Everyone had great life stories to share, and the interaction was a two-way street of experiences and lessons learned. As dire as my situation was at the time, many on the staff had personal or family stories to share that were worse than what I was enduring. This knowledge allowed me to put my personal woes into perspective and not only maintain the appreciation of life itself, but amplify my positive attitude toward the entire experience.

By the end of the second day, I had learned every one's name, details of their families, where they were from, their work history, and personal aspirations. This was not only the right thing to do, but also made those four to five days of chemo injections more memorable, allowed them to pass quickly and introduced me to new relationships with many great people. I continued being kind and engaged with everyone for the entire six months of treatment.

I learned early in this process all the intricate details regarding the varying rules for patient treatments which were different depending on which wing or floor you stayed. I soon became a subject matter expert on what exactly had to be done, and when. The rules were reminiscent of those in the military where occasional exceptions were allowed or waivers given to many supposedly steadfast rules. In my current situation – if I was healthy with my blood counts and vitals (temperature, blood pressure and heart rate) – I only needed to be checked every four to six hours. Furthermore, the required daily draw of my blood to be analyzed did not have to be between the nurses' midnight and five am mandate, but could be taken at any time during the day.

Having this newly found knowledge allowed me to develop my pitch and ultimately convince the staff that the success of my treatment, as all the doctors said, was dependent of my getting more sleep so I could stay active and exercise during the day. But I could only sleep through the night if they would adjust their rigid floor protocols. The nurses finally acquiesced and permitted my protocol to be rescheduled. During this process, I got to know a lot of great people, and after my first weekly session, I also had seven hours of uninterrupted sleep each night during my next seven week long sessions.

I was always tired and physically crushed from the effects of the chemo, but that was never an excuse for not having a positive attitude, being friendly, and thinking of others. A different mindset would never have allowed me to exercise every day, which in turn enabled me to always have my chemo sessions begin sooner than planned. Having that condensed schedule of treatment was intense on my body, but aided in the remission of my cancer.

Military Chaplain

For centuries the infantry has walked into battle or to outlying fields and woods to train for war. Even when there were wagons that were used by the Romans up to the American Civil War, or with the advent of modern transportation at the turn of the twentieth century, one of the most common means of transportation was still the soldier's boots on the ground. In the infantry, road marches or forced marches are used not only as a form of exercise, but also a common means of transportation. When we went to the field or woods to train, we would walk with everything we needed for the next week or two stuffed into large rucksacks strapped to our backs.

There was never an issue walking fifteen or twenty miles at a brisk pace to start a training exercise. We hadn't done anything yet, and all knew the forced march would be over in a few hours. Then later in the exercise, we would conduct other long forced marches between training sites and these became a bit more challenging because we were sleep deprived. Even these long marches were still not an issue unless it was at night. During these night movements part of our route might be on sandy or muddy tank trails, and we would have to navigate the deep ruts left by the heavy Abrams tanks or unseen rocks. By this time, we were tired from days of training, and our brains were not crisp or clear. For a soldier, falling flat on his face with sixty to one-hundred pounds strapped to his back was not uncommon.

Late one night, we were ending days of training in the field, everyone tired and smoked, and many with some ache or pain. The movement back to the barracks was going to be a twenty-mile night forced march at a rapid pace. Getting close to the end of this movement, we were walking up a very long, steep hill. Several soldiers had dropped out of formation and were being passed by the rest of us. We always had a vehicle trailing behind us at the end of the formation to pick up any of the injured or stragglers. That said, unless you were injured to the point of going to the hospital, no one ever wanted to see

ANOTHER BATTLE TO WIN

soldiers get on the truck for that was viewed as a weakness, a sign of quitting.

On this particular march, I was fine though feeling some pain like everyone else. Then all of a sudden out of nowhere, our chaplain, the oldest soldier in the unit, walked up next to me and said, "What a beautiful morning, soldier." I lifted my head, looked up to see a faint light coming through the trees, and then over at his inspiring grin. The only reply I could muster was, "Yes, sir, it surely is." Then he was gone, surging forward to talk to the next soldier. I looked around at some of the other soldiers who were watching him as he walked up the middle of our formation that had us hugging each side of a muddy dirt road. I saw the same reaction on their faces that I was displaying – a grin and shake of the head in disbelief at the positive attitude of our old but inspirational chaplain. I always wondered how many soldiers he prevented from falling out of formation or getting on the trailing truck. Maybe none, since all who were going to quit, had already. Regardless, he brought a smile to many of us. My pains were quickly forgotten, and it was a great start to a new day for many of us.

BE POSITIVE

Success in any endeavor is the result of a person's actions, but sustained success comes with the help of others. Have a kind heart, help those in need, and find ways to engage people in a positive manner. People like and are willing to help those who are kind, courteous, and respectful. Furthermore, we may live in a large world, but our actions, both positive and negative, will be viewed by many. There are dozens of examples where the most unexpected person whom you've had some minor interaction with and might not even remember will have a significant impact on your life plans.

Every day have a goal of making three people remember you. Say "hi" or "how are you?". Congratulate someone or tell someone that what they are doing is great. Striking up these conversations not only can make someone else's day better, but at a minimum every day you will know you had some positive impact on society. In addition, over time you will find some of these random interactions will ultimately lead to some form of relationship that will be mutually beneficial.

When you get mad, don't spout off and say what you want during the heated moment. You will undoubtedly feel great at

ANOTHER BATTLE TO WIN

the time for saying what you feel in that tense situation, but almost always will later regret what you said or how it was relayed. Wait forty-eight hours until you have calmed down and are less emotional. If the situation still warrants a response, then consider the best way to communicate your feelings.

My conclusion is simple: Always have a positive attitude and be kind to everyone, every day.

EIGHT

Learn to Sell

Kai Blacktop Sealing

Contrary to what many believe, selling is a learned skill and not blessed upon you at birth. Everything you plan to achieve in life will involve selling your ideas to someone. True, we know the success stories of companies that introduced a new product which revolutionized how we live and grabbed market share in what seems like a heartbeat.

ANOTHER BATTLE TO WIN

These are a rarity, however, and needed much less time spent on actually selling the product to the public than most products, as once advertising sparked the public's interest in the new blockbuster, the new gadget virtually sold itself. In comparison, almost every business and most people have to convince others to use their service or product and, more importantly, be able to persuade others why they should be trusted.

During college, a friend, Jim Mynhier, and I started a business we called Kai Blacktop Sealing. Our service applied a thick, black, paint-type coating to asphalt. Almost no one seals their own blacktop driveway, and if they do, most will never do it a second time. It is a physical, hot, sweaty and grimy job. If you have an accident or mishap and spill the black sealer on concrete or brick, it will be stained for years. Your clothes and shoes are permanently ruined within minutes, and the vapors from the sealer cause first degree burns. For these reasons, almost everyone who needed blacktop sealing was very receptive to having someone else do the work for them.

That said, we were 20-year-olds, not seasoned professionals in this line of work. Why would older adult homeowners ever trust young college kids who could potentially damage the appearance of their single greatest asset, their house? That rightfully-placed concern would be the greatest hurdle we had to overcome. We had to convince adult homeowners and businesses not only why our service and product were better than our competition's, but more challenging why they should trust us when we were younger than their own children.

To be successful, we had to become subject matter experts on the product and process used to seal these asphalt surfaces. In addition, we had to know and understand the decision-making process of our potential customer. Why they chose asphalt over concrete, how often they sealed this surface, was it DIY (do it yourself), or did they hire a service? Finally, we learned everything possible regarding our competition's product, service, process, price, and reputation.

There were no books or articles written on this subject to teach us or even give us a start. To gather this critical information, we talked to several individuals who had performed the service. In particular, we spent hours talking with a friend of friend who was currently paying for his education via his own blacktop sealing business in a distant

Ohio city. His breadth of knowledge related to all the key components of this service was extensive. Furthermore, knowing we would never be his competition, he shared all that he had experienced. The lessons learned regarding the best product and process and his detailed knowledge of the customer's needs were invaluable and instrumental in how we marketed and sold our service.

We then researched our competition in regard to product quality and price, including what it would cost homeowners to do it themselves. We knew that we would have to provide a great finished product – a surface that was adhesive, durable to weather, and appealing in appearance, all while charging a competitive price.

We bought only the highest quality sealer in bulk, 500 gallons at a time, directly from a manufacturer, which dramatically lowered our cost. Our expenses which included the labor to complete a driveway were half of what the homeowner would pay just for the inferior materials they could purchase at the local hardware store. In addition, we added sand to our high-end sealer which produced a more adhesive and longer lasting surface. Our product was superior to the sealer used by our competition.

LEARN TO SELL

The details we garnered from our industry expert friend, in addition to other sources, provided the foundation of our business plan. We became an authority regarding the best product, process, and competition. Now it was time to sell our service and learn firsthand more about our customer.

To market our service, we had a printing shop produce hi-end flyers and brochures. These brochures or pitch books showed the before-and-after photos of the first job we completed, which was a friend's parking lot. We included photos of our competitors' completed jobs which showed that we had a better finished surface or product. To sell our service we knew that in-person or face to face encounter with the customer generated the greatest success. Thus, we went door to door in the wealthier neighborhoods. We also had college friends use our brochures and approach to pre-sell our service in their nearby towns, and we would pay them a commission for each lead that became a client.

The first impression being of such importance in any sale forced us to not only dress as professionals, but to rehearse our sales pitch prior to every marketing trip. Once the potential client's door opened, we looked and maintained eye contact all while displaying warm and genuine smiles. We used our marketing brochures and rehearsed spiel to highlight the benefits of our product and then asked each prospect if they would like a free quote.

After every job we completed, we would hang a rope across the driveway with an attached sign and phone number to call. This simple act not only kept traffic off the surface until the sealer dried, but advertised our recently completed job in a neighborhood that we had already given several quotes to others. We would then follow up with everyone that we had met before and direct their attention to the recently completed neighbor's driveway.

All the clients were our parents' age or older, and we sold them not only on the finished product, but more importantly on the two of us. We gave them a great product at a good price. Moreover, we won numerous commercial jobs versus our much larger and more established competition, and best of all we ended up paying for our college education in the process.

Though we never figured out how to avoid getting those brutal first-degree vapor burns, we did learn how to sell ourselves.

Unless you are a monk, you will be selling something, including yourself, your entire life. At a minimum, selling starts as a kid trying to convince parents and continues with trying to influence an adult partner. Selling is a skill that you can use forever. Take the needed time to learn how to sell!

Kelly

Mine is not the only experience to learn from. Here's a story worth considering.

Kelly graduated from a great university with a business degree in marketing and a high GPA. In addition to being a stand-out high school athlete, she was smart, driven, charismatic, and always positive. She should have gotten several offers of employment after college graduation, but it was 2009 and companies were shedding employees in record numbers due to the financial crisis of 2008. Given the economic conditions at the time, Kelly took a job in our institutional equity sales and trading department as a coordinator or assistant. Over the next three years, she continually sold her skills, work ethic, and character to others with a goal of doing what few had done in our industry.

ANOTHER BATTLE TO WIN

Although she only had an undergraduate degree and minimal knowledge of finance, Kelly dreamed of becoming an institutional equity salesperson or trader. As a coordinator, Kelly worked with a team of five sales people. She was responsible for arranging, organizing, and logistically planning all aspects of her teams' institutional meetings, which numbered in the hundreds each month. These were full-day trips we sponsored between our institutional clients and our firm's research analysts or the senior management of companies we covered with research. Twelve months after her start, she had mastered the requirements of the position.

As the U.S. economy continued to struggle, Kelly focused on how she could help her team. She was always in the office before the other coordinators and one of the last to leave. Daily she was looking for ways to add value to her teammates and put their success over her own. Positive attitudes are infectious, and hers carried over to not just her teammates, but to all in the department. Her enthusiasm was often tested, but never diminished.

Our industry historically only hired MBAs from the higher ranked schools to fill equity sales or trading positions. Our department had recently begun trialing the concept of junior sales people who only had undergraduate degrees and had recently graduated. It was our team that requested a change to protocol and hired a recent undergraduate over the objections of others in our department. That newer hire was producing outstanding results and performing well ahead of expectations; with that good experience to point to, we approached Kelly to apply for another position on the Midwest team.

Over a three-month period, Kelly spent all of her free time after work and on weekends preparing for the upcoming interviews. These would be heavily focused on the stock market, detailed financial metrics of individual companies, and how we added value for our clients. She also needed to become a subject matter expert with our product. Kelly practiced for weeks in simulated interviews with several of the salespeople and subsequently did great in the interview process. Her preparation, work ethic, attitude, and consistently adding value to her team in the prior two years had built a large number of supporters, but nevertheless there were a couple of senior salespeople who were against her move into a sales role.

ANOTHER BATTLE TO WIN

We ultimately won out, however, and were allowed to bring her onto our team. Due to the pushback from the doubters, her title had to be "marketing coordinator," and not "equity sales." To us the title was irrelevant, but it appeased the naysayers and allowed Kelly to join our team.

Over the next twelve months Kelly's actions were a marvel to watch, and her contributions were what we had seen from a distance for two years. Of the roughly one hundred people working in our room, she was always the first in and the last to leave. Her positive can-do attitude continued to be seen throughout the entirety of each day. She would frequently ask each teammate how she could help and then add more value in her actions than what was expected. All the while, she was being a sponge and ramping up her knowledge base during her non-work time to add value to our clients. She spent a substantial amount of time learning how to sell to our clients, reading numerous sales books, shadowing other sales people on trips, listening to client calls, and role playing the sales process.

After a year in her official "marketing coordinator" position on our team, she had sold herself to all, including senior management. Then we were finally allowed to officially make her a junior salesperson and assign her accounts to cover.

Over the next several years, Kelly became one of the top sales people not only in the department but in the industry. Her clients consistently and broadly ranked her among the best in their sales coverage. They viewed her contributions to their process as being substantially more value-added than those of the dozens of older MBA competitors she was competing against for market share. Kelly had learned to not only successfully sell herself and gain the support of her most ardent of doubters, but also to sell a complex product in a very competitive industry.

Another great example of someone selling something with low odds of success was my daughter, Lauren selling her skills in an attempt to get a full-time job after college. During college she had spent hours preparing for every conceivable question she would be asked in interviews. She then spent more time practicing the interview process of questions and answers. These first two steps in themselves enabled her to get a full-time internship and also a short-term internship in a very competitive industry. During both internships she always treated everyone she met as if they were her future boss or most important client. Then near the end of each internship she sent a hand written thank you note to each person she had met. She received a full-time job offer from both firms: she was the only one of ten interns at the short-term internship to receive a job offer. Her approach of sending a handwritten thank you note to every person she met was the overriding reason that she was offered a full-time job.

Regardless of the profession you pursue, take the time to learn how to sell. Read articles and at least one book on the subject. Then practice with your friends or family. Learning to sell and especially selling yourself will not only shorten the time you spend in reaching your goals, it can also provide other benefits that you never expected.

Sales is a well-researched subject with significant information to enlighten your interest and expand your skills. Until you do your own research and develop your own style of selling, here are some basic thoughts that will help you sell any product, service, or even your own skill sets.

First, remember sales is a numbers game with a small percentage saying "yes," assuming you have logically

LEARN TO SELL

presented why the client or prospect should act. You are continuously working to refine and improve your pitch or rational as to why the customer should agree or act, which will increase the percentage of yeses you will receive.

As with the blacktop sealing business or Kelly's experience, you must do extensive research, study, ask a lot of questions, and become a subject matter expert on the advantages or benefits of your product, service, or even yourself. In addition, you must know everything possible about not only your competition, but also your potential client and their decision-making process. We surprisingly learned with Kai blacktop sealing that the affluent predominately liked the appearance of asphalt and were willing to pay every other year to have it sealed and made to look new. They especially liked our product, because the sand we added made the surface more adhesive. This collective knowledge made each sale easier than otherwise and generated referral sales to their like-minded neighbors.

Be prepared for every possible question that you will be asked if you are being interviewed. Think about how you will respond to rebuttals or stalls.

ANOTHER BATTLE TO WIN

Always practice, rehearse, and role play your presentation or pitch before you ever meet the prospect. Become well-versed in your key selling points and how you are going to respond when potential clients invariably say "no," or "let me think about it." You should never just wing it!

The first impression is key and most effective when done face-to-face or in person. So, dress for the occasion, have a firm handshake, make and then maintain eye contact throughout the process.

Be observant of your surroundings. Find something in which the client has interest (such as a pet or photos of a hobby) that allows you to parley that detail into a question and easier conversation. Most people enjoy and remember a conversation that involves them doing the majority of talking, thus you need to ask a lot of questions.

If you are asked a question in which you do not know the answer, never stretch, lie or pretend that you do. That act in itself is one of the quickest ways to lose a person's trust. Simply say that you don't know but will find out the answer. Then immediately keep your commitment.

Always assume that everyone you have contact with in the sales process is part of the process and treat each as a customer. The neighbor, janitor, secretary, receptionist, child and maid can have more influence than you can imagine.

Always send a handwritten thank you note to every new customer, every person who has done something kind for you, every person who interviewed you, or simply anyone you are thinking about sending a thank you email or text. Shockingly few people do this despite that it is the right thing to do and separates you from everyone else.

One technique that you can use until you foster your own approach starts with explaining two or three key reasons why someone should act on your recommendation. Then ask them for the order or the answer you want to hear and listen intently to their response. The skillset of acute listening to the prospective client is one of the most important and also one that is usually neglected. Their comments are where you will find the answer to completing the sale. At the start you will almost always hear, "no" or "let me think about it." This initial "no" is always the true start to the sales process. Reply to any rejection or delay, with "That is a good point and I understand, but let me ask you a question." Then, ask a question to find out the true reason for their hesitation, such as "Is it the cost, the time, or that we have never done business before?" or just ask, "What is your greatest concern?" Continue to listen more than you talk and ask a lot of questions.

Next, list again the key reasons why they should act, ending with once again asking for the order or what you want to accomplish. After this second request, be silent, listen, let them talk, and many times they will acquiesce. Should they not respond to your question and remain silent, don't worry even though it will be awkward. After thirty seconds (which will feel as if an hour has passed) simply say, "Silence is usually a sign of acceptance, or yes to a question; can we now conclude the sale (a common closing technique taught in sales which works)?" You will be surprised at how many will say, "*yes* or *sure*."

Finally, continue repeating this process with the focus on listening to the client's objections and incorporating them into your key selling points. This is how you address their concerns. Yes, you will have over 95% who do not agree with your recommendation and tell you no. That said, you will have success with many that otherwise would never have occurred.

Learn to sell, as this skillset will help you succeed in your life's journey.

NINE

Exercise

They say daily exercise and a healthy diet will extend your life, and for me doing pushups regularly probably saved mine. In September, 2018, I realized while doing pushups that I was getting winded, which was unusual for me. I went to see my doctor, and she told me that I had liquid in my right lung and needed a CT Scan.

ANOTHER BATTLE TO WIN

Over the next 14 days, my diagnosis changed several times. At the start, they thought I had one type of cancer with only months to live, then a rare Non-Hodgkin's Lymphoma with a fifty percent chance of being alive in three to five years. My last doctor determined that I had a totally different type of Non-Hodgkin's Lymphoma, with a seventy percent chance of being cured.

My exercise routine likely saved my life, as it not only led to finding my cancer early, but also allowed my body to handle a more intense chemo regimen that resulted in remission of the cancer.

I'd always enjoyed exercising, but my routine became more rigorous when I prepared to join the military and during my training there. Until I joined the military, a three-mile jog and lifting weights at the gym three times a week was the pinnacle of my workout routine. To achieve my goals in the Army I knew I had to be in outstanding shape, so I trained for months. Before day one of military service, I knew I would have to be able to walk at a fast pace for twenty miles, while carrying seventy to eighty pounds of gear. My run times would need to be below thirteen minutes for a two-mile run and thirty-five minutes for a five-mile run. Being able to do

EXERCISE

ten dead hanging pullups and eighty sit-ups and pushups each in two minutes were the minimum thresholds. I trained until I could surpass those levels. What I didn't know at the time was that once I was actually in the Army those tasks were going to be performed on little to no sleep and with an aching body.

When I reported for military duty and the training started, the standard routine for every course or class quickly became apparent. The instructors would smoke us with extreme exercises the night before we took our first APFT. They had us doing endless pushups and sit-ups mixed with other exercises for upwards of one hour. The result was always the same – we would be tired and sore before the next morning's test.

When we were just getting smoked or thrashed as punishment for some screw up, we always did pushups, flutter kicks and some cardio exercise, such as low crawling through the mud. The instructors always stopped when half of our group had collapsed to the mud or pavement. The biggest benefit from my months of preparation was that during the first eighteen months of service, I was always being subjected to long periods of exercise as punishment with a large group of soldiers. I quickly learned that even though I was much

ANOTHER BATTLE TO WIN

older than my peers, given my physical condition, I was always in the top quartile of any group. These thrashings would be over long before I suffered any real pain. The physical conditioning also allowed me to score near the top on all my APFTs, which aided me in passing several challenging courses or in receiving sought-after duty assignments.

After the military, I made the effort to exercise every day, even during the seventy days a year that I was traveling and sleeping in a hotel. The daily exercise provided the extra energy that allowed me to work longer hours and have greater success than I might have otherwise.

Daily exercise in any form always results in something positive. It saved my life in finding my cancer early and probably prevented me from being seriously injured during my military service.

Exercise every day. Start today, and continue for the rest of your life.

TEN

Do the Right Thing

No matter where you are, no matter what stage of life you are at, no matter what you are doing or with whom, you will be challenged to make moral and ethical decisions. You might be in a leadership position or you might not, but your choices should always be ones you can stand behind and be proud of.

ANOTHER BATTLE TO WIN

Offerings in Equity Capital Markets

During my years spent working in equity capital markets, my firm was involved in hundreds of offerings for newly issued shares of a company's stock. Multiple departments and dozens of people from our firm were involved in each offering where we were the lead manager. The lead manager or underwriter had the greatest responsibility for getting the deal done and would also be getting paid the greatest amount of money if successful. Individual's annual bonus could be impacted by tens, if not hundreds of thousands of dollars from just one lead managed offering or deal. This large amount of money being paid to the firm, and individuals, meant there was risk that someone would not do the right thing.

All of Wall Street's broker dealers or investment banks, including my firm, represented not only the company selling these newly issued shares, but also had relationships with the professional institutional investors who were the buyers of these shares. These offerings could be for five to twenty million shares of stock, so even a fifty-cent fluctuation in price could be worth millions of dollars to the company issuing shares and hundreds of thousands of dollars in fees to the investment bank.

The investment banker's client relationship was with the company issuing the new shares. The company wanted the highest price possible. The investment banker's annual bonus was roughly eighty percent of their total compensation and based predominately on the fees generated from these offerings. On average, a banker did two to three deals a year. For them, successfully getting their offering done was a must. They also wanted the highest possible price, which would benefit their client and their own year-end bonus.

I was in the equity sales department, and our clients were the professional institutional buyers. They were the mutual funds, state pension plans, or investment advisors who actually managed stock portfolios. Unlike our investment banking counterparts, we interacted and were informally evaluated by our clients on a daily basis. A portion of our compensation was from commissions generated from these offerings. A client getting a large allocation on a single deal could be financially significant for us. That said, if the offering was priced inappropriately by our bankers and did not trade

ANOTHER BATTLE TO WIN

well after the deal, we would be in the doghouse with our client. Many times, our punishment would be no regular trading for weeks or even months. Thus, any economic benefit sales received from the client participating and being given a large allocation of newly issued shares of stock would be dwarfed by their lack of regular trading. The buyers who were our clients wanted not only the lowest price on these offerings, which benefited their investors in addition to enhancing their own performance, but also to know the true demand for the offering. Determining the real demand was subjective with multiple factors, but transparency on the varying types of institutional investors participating was of significant value. Shorter term trading-oriented hedge funds created a higher degree of potential volatility versus long term buy and hold mutual funds. This factor alone if fully known would have an impact on the price buyers were willing to pay for these new shares.

There was clearly a potential conflict of interest on Wall Street between the different departments within the same firm. These large fees generated some pressure from management to get the deals done. At some firms you could lose your job if you provided too much transparency on what other institutions were saying, what you thought of senior management after traveling with them on their marketing road show, or the investment style of institutions who had orders in the book for the offering. At many firms, these actions would result in you being told you weren't a team player, and you could expect a smaller year-end bonus. My firm was one of few firms on Wall Street that allowed sales and research to give their personal opinion and provide greater transparency to our institutional clients without fear of retribution. Our comments to the buyers could result in the deal being priced lower than expected, which meant less money for the issuing company and lower fees to our firm.

In business as elsewhere, tell the truth. Don't exaggerate. Don't manipulate. You may upset a friend, relative or your boss, but always do the right thing.

Fines in Equity Capital Markets

Almost all of Wall Street, including our department, paid the majority of each person's yearly compensation as a subjective bonus at the start of the following year. Given this subjective nature, some individuals would attempt to take credit for revenues that they believed that they, versus other co-workers, were largely responsible for generating.

These individuals were trying to benefit financially over others who might actually be more deserving. The industry spent a considerable amount of time to make the compensation process as fair and objective as possible, but determining bonuses is still a subjective process. Every firm operates differently, though the vast majority of the mid to large sized firms function as a team effort. Though there is always a lead banker, or salesperson, there are actually many people working on providing service to each client. This is clearly the right approach for multiple reasons and when it's working properly results in providing the client with the best service. Often, individuals who are in support roles add significant value to the clients, though their support contributions are usually not visible to most observers. Unlike most of the employees in equity capital markets, these support individuals are salaried employees and do not fully participate in the larger bonuses paid at year end. They are very important to the process: their actions are typically client-focused and not self-serving. Nevertheless, occasionally someone on the support staff was not treated with the respect they deserved.

Our firm was known for having a great culture, working as a team, and not hiring or retaining assholes. As a department of roughly three hundred people, we usually only had one person every other year who could not grasp the concept of true team play. They would put their own interests ahead of their teammates. Unfortunately, sometimes their behavior would result in the charge of "emotional insensitivity" or sometimes they would be guilty of disrespecting someone on the support staff, or even another teammate who was critical to our overall success. On these occasions the person would not only be counseled to change their behavior, but fined upwards of five percent of their annual compensation. That may not sound like much, but telling someone they are going to make $15 - 25,000 less for not doing the right thing helped to change behavior.

Sadly, though, most firms don't have a "no asshole" policy. Even some of the most admired companies will at times tolerate selfish individuals or jerks if they generate significant revenue for that firm. Fines can and will change behavior for a while, but too often the underlying core of the person persists. That person needs an epiphany moment, such as being terminated, to enact true behavioral change.

I knew of two individuals who were fined for not being respectful to others. They both acted better for a period of time but remained self-centered individuals. Both lost tens of thousands of dollars in annual compensation and sucked time and energy from their co-workers who had to deal daily with their actions. One of those individuals was passed over for a major, life-altering promotion because of their actions and personality.

When you are considering joining a firm, how can you know if someone on the team is a jerk or the work environment is not as it is purported? Don't be shy. Ask as many of the people as possible who work at the firm for their opinion. Talk to peers, subordinates, secretaries, suppliers and management. Ask as many questions as they have time for and are willing share. What do they like most and least about their job, peers, and management? If they could change anything in the organization what would that be? What do they tell their partner or best friend about the organization, boss, or other teammates? You will be surprised by how much you will learn about an organization or individuals by listening to others. If you only find one or two people complaining, they usually are the problem.

Before taking a job, or deciding on a new hire, take extra time to reach your conclusion. Make sure that the work environment is healthy. Especially be confident that your boss is a team player and mentor. The compensation may be great, or the new hire a rainmaker, but working in a poorly managed organization or with a bad apple will always overwhelm any financial benefit you receive.

Army National Training Center

In the Army, both on the battlefield and the training grounds, doing the right thing means going beyond your own personal interest to looking out for the team as a whole.

The National Training Center or NTC is a massive, sprawling Army base located in the middle of the desert at Ft. Irwin, CA. This base is roughly five hours south of Las Vegas, NV, where some of the most realistic training in the Army is conducted every month on its desert floors. All of the Army's

ANOTHER BATTLE TO WIN

infantry divisions rotate their brigades of roughly 2000 men into Fort Irwin every three years for a month of war games against the world class OPFOR, or Opposing Force. The Opposing Force is an Army unit of infantry and armor soldiers whose intimate knowledge of the terrain and monthly battles against our nation's warriors provides them with a significant competitive advantage. In January of 1995 it was our turn, and 1st Brigade, 24th Infantry was augmented by other support units, such as air defense, field artillery, and a battalion of infantry from the 82nd Airborne Division.

These war games are monitored, evaluated, and recorded via satellite; the games include embedded evaluators from the training center. Those in more senior leadership positions are continuously evaluated on their performance and these reviews are of significant value in many ways. This feedback can be used in each officer and non-commissioned officer's annual evaluation report. The emotions encompassing these annual evaluations were similar to Wall Street's annual subjective bonus. These annual reports determine how fast officers and non-commissioned officers get promoted versus their peers, and in some cases, whether they are even allowed to remain in the Army. Unfortunately, some individuals focus more on their own personal victories while at the National Training Center, and not the great lessons to be absorbed from this unique experience.

NTC rotations all start as ours did, which was the challenge to draw or pick your vehicles from the central pool of equipment. Their equipment, such as Bradley Fighting Vehicles, or Abrams tanks were all old, overused, and in poor mechanical condition. We had to fix all the deficiencies before we could start our training. Then we moved to the firing ranges to zero, or calibrate, our weapon systems, and we practiced our movements through the desert. We would spend several days on the main base sleeping in pup tents before we began our two weeks of mock battles in the surrounding desert.

All of the leadership with the rank of captain or above had individual monitors assigned to shadow them. These leaders were assessed or evaluated on a daily basis. The assessments would be shared daily during our open forum AARs which included all the officers and senior enlisted soldiers and could number upwards of 150 leaders. Here we openly discussed in excruciating detail the actions of the day, what we did well, and what we needed to improve. Everyone knew during these open critiques that their performance during these weeks of training would be a major component of their next annual review.

The harsh terrain and climate at NTC, coupled with training that was simulated to be as close as possible to combat, were factors that increased stress on our leadership. Elevating the stress was one of the intents of these exercises, as stress affected everyone: it is contagious and trickles down to the lowest level. Add in the leaders who had their own performance review as a focus, and soldiers quickly saw who were the good leaders that cared more about their men than their own personal success.

Our company commander would openly talk with the three of us lieutenants about his officer evaluation report and the need for all to achieve a high rating. Our battalion commander's actions while on base, had all the junior officers and senior enlisted soldiers convinced that his own annual review was more important to him than our personal development. Having my two senior leaders care so much about their own annual reviews made the work environment extremely difficult. Their actions even before this rotation to NTC had demonstrated that training our soldiers for war appeared to be secondary to their looking good on paper, improving their own personal rating, and promoting their personal career advancement.

On day one at NTC, our battalion commander personally went to each of his five companies of 100 men and ordered them to set up a field arms room. It was up to each company commander to determine how the arms room would be established. The end state was for all our weapons and sensitive items to be immediately placed in some form of field arms room and kept under a 24-hour guard. He said there would be no weapons or night vision devices misplaced or lost on his watch.

Our company commander could not be found, so the order was given to First Lieutenant Chris, our executive officer, who was in charge of the company in our commander's absence. Securing under guard hundreds of sensitive items in a manner that would allow the unit to quickly draw or have each soldier get their assigned weapons left few options. Lt. Chris could have used an open section of our sleeping area and surrounded that with concertina wire, but that would not have been a secure option. He could have used a few of our pup tents and have those soldiers sleep in the open, but these two-person tents were small, and he would need many. The best and most secure option was to use our commander's larger tent, which was the size of six small pup tents. Needing to act on the battalion commander's order, having no better option, and not being able to locate our commander, Lt. Chris took command of our company commander's larger tent to use as our arms room. He then had all 100 of the company's soldiers sign in, or place their assigned weapons and other sensitive items inside. The commander's tent, or now our new field arms room, was quickly filled to its capacity, with two soldiers outside and standing tall on their guard duty. The soldiers, and especially the non-commission officers were impressed with Chris's solution. He had taken a risk for the benefit of the unit.

Our company commander finally returned only to find his tent under guard and filled with his company's sensitive items. Most would think he would have been thankful that the battalion commander's order had been fulfilled in his absence. Instead, he went ballistic and into a tirade. He yelled and verbally humiliated Lt. Chris in front of our entire company. He even went so far to say, "You will do whatever I tell you to do, and if that includes turning a wrench, then you will do it."

DO THE RIGHT THING

Lt. Chris maintained his professional demeanor during this verbal thrashing and just stood there at attention. Finally, he said, "Sir, I will only do as you say and nothing more or less." Everyone in the company knew that using the company commander's larger tent was Lt. Chris's only option, and as the acting commanding officer, he had the authority and had been ordered by our battalion commander to make a quick decision. Our entire company of soldiers saw firsthand that our commander was not acting rationally and was thinking only of himself versus the unit. Any respect he had earned from his men, other than authoritative, was now gone. In contrast to Lt. Chris, the commander was only thinking of himself.

Days later we had moved off the post and into the desert to conduct two weeks of daily mock battles. Early in the exercise, one of our assigned missions was to conduct a deliberate attack in challenging boulder-covered terrain. The quickest route to our objective was across a large open area that was surrounded by rolling hills and large boulders. Movement through the open terrain would be substantially faster and would allow us to meet the battalion commander's time line. But the plan would also put our company at great risk of being isolated by the opposing force and destroyed one by one. We three platoon leaders knew the plan to cross the open terrain was not sound, just by looking at our maps. When we mentioned to our commander the risk and inability to meet its timeline, he didn't seem concerned and only said, "This is what we are going to do, men." We had no idea if he had mentioned to the battalion commander or his staff the lunacy of their timeline or the extreme danger of crossing open terrain or was just clueless, himself.

Given our role in the mission, our commander told us not to become decisively engaged with the enemy forces. We had to get all our vehicles and men to an area just beyond the large open area in a very short period of time. Our commander, in a rare and positive display of leadership, was going to show his men that he would lead from the front. So, his Bradley Fighting Vehicle was the first vehicle to enter the open terrain. Less than one minute later, his vehicle and two others were decisively engaged and destroyed. Clearly his plan was a failure.

During our wargames, commanders were allowed to leave their destroyed vehicle and take command of another. This allows them to continue their mission and evaluation; in effect, they are given a rare second chance. Our commander's vehicle was out in the open and several hundred yards into the enemy's kill zone. Any vehicle that entered this area would be destroyed, unless the opposing forces vehicles could be located and destroyed first. The most logical decision would have been for our commander to leave his vehicle and move back under the cover of the terrain to link up with one of us. Then he could take command of one of our vehicles, inform our battalion commander of our need to enact an alternate route, and be able to command our company. But the order we heard from him over the company net, or radio, was for us to come out into the kill zone with our vehicles and pick him up.

Over the course of the next five minutes, no one would acknowledge his request. All replied that they had communication problems and that the radio transmissions were breaking up. At the same time, we began moving our men and vehicles along the sides of the open area where there was shelter from the enemy's weapon systems. Our commander had not only lost the respect of the men, but also lost his ride and second chance to complete this mission. Our commander continued to flounder for the rest of our time spent at Fort Irwin, but our battalion commander or his boss had his own performance problems and didn't notice our commander's self-centered focus or poor leadership.

In the military and team-oriented organizations, individuals who are focused on their own success, versus their team's success, become a detriment to the group. As almost all of us have seen, self-centered leaders, to the chagrin of many, can and do remain in their positions much longer than everyone imagined possible.

Leadership positions in the military follow a career path where officers are virtually guaranteed two lower level command positions as platoon leaders or commanders and company commanders. These positions change roughly every eighteen to twenty-four months and a serious infraction would have to occur for an officer to be relieved of command earlier than planned. Poor leadership or a self-centered focus is almost never a reason for relinquishing a leadership role early. Following early command positions, officers undergo years of additional training and varying support roles before being considered for their next command. Thus, those whose primary focus is on their own career can go unnoticed and even rise to take another command position as evidenced by my first battalion commander.

DO THE RIGHT THING

In business where the focus is on returns on investment, stakeholders, shareholders, and the bottom line, poor managers are eventually removed, but surprisingly they, too, can remain for much longer than anyone thought possible. There are dozens of books and thousands of examples written about leadership, yet poor leaders continue to exist. Often, senior leadership influences or even directly places a problem leader into their current role. The removal of that problem leader implies that the senior was wrong and made a mistake. Unfortunately, human nature, especially among most decision makers and alpha personalities, is to never show weakness or admit error. These decisionmakers can consistently be willing to tolerate a problem leader, ignore the pleas of many, or justify why they are right so that they don't have to acknowledge their own mistake. Normally a leader two layers or higher than the problem leader is the one to force corrective action.

Why are some individuals self-centered, prone to lie, or slightly bend the truth? Why are they willing to cheat or take shortcuts that benefit them in the short term but hurt others and are poor decisions in the long term? In fact, is it possible to be successful and advance your career as a leader while putting your team's success ahead of your own?

Starting with the later, I contend that you can have dual success, though if you take the route of honest, team-centered behavior, it may take longer for your potential to be rewarded with a higher leadership position.

A leader must already have attained a skill set and knowledge base that is at least equivalent and should surpass that of your team mates. The leader should be a contributing member of the team, setting the example and leading from the front, constantly working harder than most and allocating more time to learn more and improve. This singular focus is why a person was chosen for a leadership role.

As to why some individuals in power can be bad apples and remain in their positions or even be elevated to higher positions before they fall from grace (which they almost always do), history has shown that self-centered leaders or just bad people have always been part of society. Greed, pride, ego, and selfishness are common in most areas of leadership.

Better yet is to ask why it is that some people actually do the right thing? In my humble opinion the reason is a combination of our genetic make-up in addition to the work of our parents, teachers, and religious community instilling and continually reinforcing the key principles of right and wrong. Then as we grow into adults, the best among us have the maturity and self-awareness to follow the appropriate path while accepting the consequences of their mistakes and learning from them.

Regardless of whether you're in a leadership role or not, think of the following:

Always push yourself to be the best at whatever you do and maintain an elevated skillset so that you are worthy of a leadership position and contributing to your teams' success.

Put your subordinates' well-being ahead of your own.

Explain to your team what you are doing and why.

But even when you are not in a leadership position, yourself, do the right thing.

Work to remove all bias and you will be surprised to learn who are the best leaders and stars of your organization. They are almost never the loudest, who lack confidence, or the silver-tongued who, lacking integrity, will say anything, or the

ANOTHER BATTLE TO WIN

self-acknowledged strongest, who rarely will be the ones covering your back in the thick of confrontation.

Trust is a two-way street and has to be earned, but give everyone a chance and the benefit of the doubt. Their own actions will quickly confirm or deny if you can trust them. This more trusting attitude makes life easier and less stressful. You will marvel at some you initially questioned who prove to be the most trustworthy.

Ethics matters in the workplace, on battlefield, and at home to you and your team as a whole. You will be surprised how often you will be asked to work in the gray area. Many times, it will be to cover for someone's mistake, or sometimes to make you or someone else look good, or sometimes to provide a short-term win for the team or organization. These short-term benefits derived from conspicuously doubtful actions are almost always an underlying cancer to the organization.

Live a life of integrity, even when your actions cause you short term pain. You may not get the promotion or the great next job in your organization because you have character. That said, you will be able to look at yourself in the mirror with peace of mind and sleep better at night. You will learn over time that many are watching, and you will earn the respect of others for your actions.

Always ask yourself before you conduct an act that could be interpreted as questionable "Would I want to read about this, with my name attached to the action in the newspaper or on-line?" Character, and how you have helped others in life, will be how you are remembered once you are gone.

Don't ever lie, as you do not need to bend the truth to convince others. They might not like what you are saying, but if they are honest, themselves, they will be supportive, understanding, and respectful of your honesty.

Keep your promises, and make your commitment mean something.

Strive to be a confident professional.

Be humble, never boisterous or arrogant.

When you are wrong, don't get defensive or shift the blame. As difficult as it is, own up or apologize immediately. When at a loss for words, just use the Marine Corps technique and say, "My bust."

Conclusion

Having just finished my fourth life challenge in the battle with cancer, I'm about to start the next chapter in my life. A month after my eighth and last session of chemotherapy, my doctor explained the next phase of my treatment. He said I would undergo maintenance therapy for the next two years, which would improve my odds of the cancer not recurring. The process would consist of taking chemo pills daily, once a month getting an injection of the chemo related drug Vincristine, and five days of steroids. That was the easy part, as he quietly mentioned that I would also be getting get my favorite Lumbar Push, or injection of Methotrexate into my spine every three months. They would check for cancer every few months with a PET Scan.

He asked if I had any plans, and I told him we were going to Florida for the month of April. He looked shocked when I told him we were driving, so I asked if that was ok. He said I would be very tired and should fly, but if I was going to drive, to plan for extra time. We made the 24-hour drive in two days, and regardless of how I felt, it was great to see the different scenery that I had missed the prior six months. Once we got to Florida, my ignorance about the truth of his comments came full circle. Mentally I felt fine, but physically I was tired from the effects of the prior six months of treatment. I didn't set an alarm clock the entire trip and ended up sleeping nine hours each day.

In Florida, I started thinking about life after cancer, and given this disease could come back, what was next? Two years before being diagnosed, I had left my firm following twenty years of institutional equity sales. At that time, I was ready for a change, which included travel and then trading stocks in our basement. Following the market and researching new stock ideas to buy or short is what I enjoyed and was a version of what I had been doing professionally. Working from home also included freedom from the corporate bureaucracy. But I had substantially less daily interaction with others, substantially fewer challenges, substantially less stimulation. I wasn't sure what was next, but after sitting alone in front of computer screens to trade stocks, that was not top of my list of activities to pursue.

There is a reasonable chance that the next endeavor will be different from what I know. At the age of fifty-nine, I will once again be starting all over. At what age, after how many life challenges, are we done pushing ourselves to win our next battle? Personally, I don't believe there is an age when we are too old or a point in time when it is too late to face any crisis or chase your dream. There is nothing that we cannot achieve if we take the necessary actions and are willing to pay the price. Every battle has already been successfully overcome by someone and we should take heart from that.

Recommended Reading

Equity Markets:

How to Make Money in the Stock Market	William O'Neil
Reminiscences of a Stock Operator	Edwin Lafevre
How to Trade Stocks	Jesse Livermore
Complete Turtle Traders	Richard Dennis
Little Book that Beats the Market	Joel Greenblatt
The Little Book of Market Wizards (traders)	Jack D. Schwager
Technical Analysis & Stock Trends	Robert Edwards
	John McGee
Financial Analysis of the Financial Markets	John Murphy
Trading to Win	Ari Kiev

Business:

Think and Grow Rich	Napoleon Hill
How to Win Friends and Influence People	Dale Carnegie
7 Habits of Highly Effective People	Stephen Covey
Make Your Bed	W. McRaven
Mind Gym	Gary Mack

Extreme Ownership	Jocko Willink
Slight Edge	Jeff Olson
Outsiders	W. Thorndyke
Greatest Salesman in the World	Og Mandino
How to Master the Art of Selling	Tom Hopkins
The Art of Closing Any Deal	James W. Pickens

Military:

Marine, the Life of Chesty Puller	Burke Davis
Attacks	Irwin Rommel
Red Platoon	Clinton Romesha
Gates of Fire	Steven Pressfield
Back in the Fight	J. Kapaziewski
Ghost Soldiers	Hampton Sides
Flags of Our Fathers	James Bradley
Band of Brothers	Steven Ambrose
Starship Troopers	George Heinlein
Duffers Drift	Ernest Swinton
The Defense of Hill 781	J. McDonough
Killer Angels	Michael Shaara
We Were Soldiers Once & Young	Harold Moore
Rubicon	Tom Holland
The Art of War	Sun Tzu
On War	Clausewitz

Acknowledgements

I want to thank Mary Basson (author of *Saving Kandinsky*) or "Peetie" whose patience and brilliance in editing made this book better than it otherwise would have been.

In addition, I want to thank the many friends, coworkers, soldiers and doctors whose character and actions are the basis of many of the stories. Though I have changed your names and there are some who go unnamed, I hope you know who you are and how much you have meant to me.

Finally, I want to thank all of those who have served or are serving. Anything that I have endured pales in comparison to so many of your experiences.

Made in the USA
Monee, IL
30 December 2019